THE GREAT COMPOSERS
THEIR LIVES AND TIMES

Jacques
Offenbach
1819-1880

Johann
Strauss II
1825-1899

Claude
Debussy
1862-1918

Maurice
Ravel
1875-1937

Staff Credits

Editors
Laura Buller
David Buxton

Art Editors
Helen James
Debbie Jecock

Deputy Editor
Barbara Segall

Sub-editors
Geraldine Jones
Judy Oliver
Nigel Rodgers

Designers
Steve Chilcott
Shirin Patel
Chris Rathbone

Picture Researchers
Georgina Barker
Julia Calloway
Vanessa Cawley

Production Controllers
Deborah Cracknell
Sue Fuller

Secretary
Lynn Small

Publishing Director
Reg Wright

Managing Editor
Sue Lyon

Consultants
Dr Antony Hopkins
Commander of the Order
of the British Empire
Fellow of the
Royal College of Music

Nick Mapstone BA, MA

Keith Shadwick BA

Reference Edition Published 1990

Published by Marshall Cavendish Corporation
147 West Merrick Road
Freeport, Long Island
N.Y. 11520

Typeset by Maclink, Hull
Printed by Times Offset Private Ltd.,
Singapore

© Marshall Cavendish Limited MCMLXXXIV,
MCMLXXXVII, MCMXC

Library of Congress Cataloging-in-Publication Data

The Composers: the great composers, their lives and times.
p. ca.
Cover title: Great composers II.
ISBN 1-85435-300-4 (set): $175.00
1. Composers—Biography.   2. Music appreciation.
I. Marshall Cavendish Corporation.
II. Title: Great composers II.
ML390.C7185 1990   780'.92'2—dc20 [B]   89-23988

ISBN 1-85435-300-4 (set)   CIP
1-85435-301-2 (vol)   MN

THE GREAT COMPOSERS
THEIR LIVES AND TIMES

Jacques
Offenbach
1819-1880

Johann
Strauss II
1825-1899

Claude
Debussy
1862-1918

Maurice
Ravel
1875-1937

MARSHALL CAVENDISH
NEW YORK · LONDON · SYDNEY

Preface
by Antony Hopkins

Radio Times

There is an old nursery rhyme whose final line is 'she shall have music wherever she goes'. Today, 'she' has become 'we', for music is so much a part of everyday life that it is almost unavoidable: it accompanies us as we pick our way along the crowded aisles of the supermarket; it deafens us at cocktail parties; it marks time as we wait at airports; and it is even used in dentists' surgeries to calm our apprehension. The danger of such over-exposure is that we begin to treat music as one of those taken-for-granted amenities like electric light or central heating – we may be aware of it but we take little notice. We hear but we do not listen. Now it is true that a great deal of such music makes no real demands, even though the performances have a highly professional gloss. It has been described as 'wallpaper music' and, though wallpaper can be an asset to a room, it is scarcely a major art-form. But music of quality does make demands and it deserves more than casual listening, as it is a language of extraordinary power and subtlety. And it is a truly international language, for if you look in record shops in any of the five continents you will see many of the same works – works that are universally loved and that have retained their appeal over the centuries. Great music is also the nearest equivalent we have to a time machine, since every performance enables us to experience the emotions of people long dead; we can share Bach's faith, Haydn's wit, Beethoven's adversity, and Liszt's grand passions.

While music of quality may make an immediate emotional appeal, our enjoyment will be greatly enhanced if we can cultivate a keener sense of period, for the language of music undergoes continual change. Mozart does not 'speak' to us in the same way as Brahms, though both composers may be concerned to express the same truths. To understand such differences, we need to know something about the background to composers' lives, their position in society, the reception accorded to their music, their loves, their triumphs and disasters. It is in these areas that GREAT COMPOSERS: THEIR LIVES AND TIMES is so enlightening. Written in an eminently readable style, free from jargon and pedantry, this unique series sheds a clear light on all aspects of a composer's life, works and times, so that we know him like a personal friend. This greater knowledge and understanding will undoubtedly bring a fuller enjoyment and appreciation of music's riches, teaching us how much it has to offer if we listen rather than hear.

Antony Hopkins

Antony Hopkins is best known for his radio programme, **Talking about Music**, but he has also composed film scores, incidental music and operas. He holds an honorary Doctorate at Stirling University and Fellowships at Robinson College, Cambridge and at the Royal College of Music. In 1976 he was made a Commander of the British Empire.

THE
GREAT COMPOSERS
THEIR LIVES AND TIMES

Contents

Introduction

The mid-19th century was an age of greater awareness of all the arts. The increasing wealth of the lower and middle classes resulted in a demand for accessible musical and theatrical entertainment and a growth of theatres and concert halls. Revolutions in road and rail transport and the great World Exhibitions brought closer a world of new artistic and muscial influences. The four composers in this volume drew upon these new influences, developing characteristic and highly personal styles.

Jacques Offenbach responded to the growing need for popular music, writing in a light but elegant style that seemed to epitomize the spirit of an exuberant, carefree Paris. His work in Les Bouffes-Parisiens made his name synonymous with French operetta. Just as the music of

Offenbach is unmistakably the music of Paris, so the sparkling waltzes of Johann Strauss II paint a perfect musical picture of Vienna. Strauss was undoubtedly the waltz king, but dancers often stopped still, captured by his heady, exciting music.

As the century progressed, composers were greatly influenced by artistic movements outside music. Claude Debussy turned to Impressionism and Symbolism in painting and literature. The result was a musical 'impressionism', in which he created original and highly evocative music of great emotional power.

Debussy's innovative style opened new doors for other composers, including his contemporary, Maurice Ravel. The romance of Spain was a notion that influenced many French artists, but it was Ravel, above all, who captured its flavour and colour in his stirring orchestral works.

THE GREAT COMPOSERS

Jacques Offenbach

1819-1880

Jacques Offenbach was the toast of Paris in the late 19th century. Although the composer, who was later called the 'Mozart of the Champs Elysées', attended the Paris Conservatoire for one year, he learned his art by practice rather than theory. Offenbach worked in Paris theatre as both a cello virtuoso and a conductor before setting up his own venue, Les Bouffes-Parisiens. There, his humorous, witty and often satirical works dominated the Paris musical scene. An untiring impresario, Offenbach completed more than 90 works for the stage. Many celebrated in music the vivacious city of Paris, most notably in the operatic compilation of his work, Gaieté Parisienne, analysed in the Listener's Guide. *The carefree spirit of Paris was shattered by the Franco-Prussian war, as detailed in* In The Background, *but outside Paris, the sparkling success of Offenbach's works helped to establish the operetta form, and became the basis for the modern musical.*

Jacques Offenbach, the composer who so epitomized the spirit of Paris that he was called the 'Mozart of the Champs Elysées', was actually of German origin and never mastered the language of his adopted home. At 12, he was sent to France to attend the Paris Conservatoire, but Offenbach was more interested in popular music than in the 'serious' music studied there, so he left to seek work in the theatre. He played cello in several orchestras and occasionally wrote incidental music, but his reputation grew with a lucrative post at the Comédie Française. He then set up his own theatre, Les Bouffes-Parisiens. It was an outrageous success; Offenbach's witty humour, his mastery of the operetta and his vivacious music captured all of Paris for the next twenty years. He continued to work incessantly until his death in 1880.

The Mansell Collection

COMPOSER'S LIFE

' "O" de Cologne '

Of German-Jewish origins, Jacques Offenbach –
dubbed 'Monsieur "O" de Cologne' – expressed
his zest for life in the witty and typically French
world of operetta which he created.

One of Jacques Offenbach's first best-selling songs A toi *(the title page of which is shown above) was dedicated to Herminie d'Alcain, the daughter of a Parisian society hostess at whose soirées Offenbach had played. In 1844 he married Herminie and later had four children – (from left to right) Marie, Berthe, Pepita and Jacqueline.*

Offenbach was a small, eccentric-looking man with thin Jewish features, dandy whiskers and pince-nez. He had a birdlike quality about him – a bright chirpy zest for living. He was a witty talker and personally provided the source of much of the humour in his works to his librettists. He was also a compulsive worker, forever pressing his librettists for their material and driving everyone into a fever of activity. All of this was expressed in the liveliest examples of his music. Yet there is more to Offenbach than this exuberant front suggests at first sight. Underneath his lively exterior he was by nature a romantic personality, and woven into his music are characteristically tender and lyrical melodies and songs.

Though of German origin, Offenbach became as French in character as his works, yet he never mastered the French language. His musical ancestry was in the music hall song, the folksong, the opéra comique and possibly in Rossini and Mozart. In fact, it was Rossini who summed him up best and most flatteringly when he called Offenbach 'the Mozart of the Champs Elysées'.

From Germany to France

Offenbach's grandfather, Juda Eberst, a singer and music-teacher had settled in what is now a suburb of Frankfurt – Offenbach-am-Main. Juda's son Isaac inherited his father's musical inclinations, and when he left home at the age of 20 it was to a precarious life as an itinerant singer and violinist. Eventually, in 1802, Isaac settled in Deutz, a suburb of Cologne, finding there fairly regular employment with light orchestras and dance-bands. Given the nickname of 'Der Offenbacher', he adopted the name of Offenbach feeling that it had more of a musical ring to it than Eberst. In 1805 he married a local girl called Marianne Rindskopf and together they managed to make a living and raise a large family.

There were 10 children in all, and Jakob (later Jacques) born in 1819, was their seventh child. He grew up happily, went to the local school and was taught the violin by his father. It soon became clear that he had exceptional musical talents. By the time he was eight he had started to compose and at nine had chosen the cello as his special instrument. His first teacher was an eccentric Cologne professor, Josef Alexander.

Together with his brother Julius on violin and sister Isabella on piano, he formed a youthful trio and played in the local dance-halls and cafés. Their father acted as manager, and naturally enough anything they earned helped the family finances.

Isaac was determined that his children should be given every opportunity to develop their talents, so he decided to move Jakob to another teacher, Bernhard Breuer (to whom in 1833 Offenbach dedicated his Opus 1). Then, when Offenbach was 14, his father decided to send both sons to Paris to study music. An audition was arranged for them at the famous Paris Conservatoire. The Conservatoire had strict rules forbidding entry to foreign students. However, the director – Luigi Cherubini – was so impressed by Jakob's talents that he agreed to take both of the young Offenbachs as students.

However, Offenbach's interest in music more popular than that offered by the strict curriculum of the Conservatoire was strong, and he found the teaching dull and irksome. The Conservatoire was ideal for students with more serious intentions like

Henry Bright 'View of Cologne'. Oscar & Peter Johnson. The Bridgeman Art Library

asked to contribute a waltz to their repertoire. Offenbach also returned to the cello, lucratively exploiting his talents as a virtuoso performer in the salons of the nobility. For these occasions he wrote his own music and in January 1839 gave his first public concert. Later that year he was asked to write the incidental music for a comedy *Pascal et Chambord* but the production was a failure and the commission led nowhere. Luckily for the two boys their father visited them in Paris: he advised his sons to take up a plan to travel in Europe as virtuoso performers. But before this the brothers returned to Cologne for a family reunion.

Jacques returned to Paris and Jules took up a post in Bordeaux, but by the end of 1840 they were in Cologne again, this time because of more unfortunate circumstances – their brother had died and their mother was ill. Sadly, she too died while they were there.

Marriage and success

Back in Paris Offenbach fell in love with a charming girl called Herminie. But her parents were keen to see some tangible proof of his suitability as a husband and provider. He therefore organized larger concerts in Paris and introduced more of his own works, including a song that became very popular — *A toi,* (aptly dedicated to Herminie d'Alcain). He arranged tours in France and Germany and then, in 1844, went for the first time to London. Here he took part in concerts at Her Majesty's Theatre and played at Court for Queen Victoria and Prince Albert. He returned from his London success a wealthy young man and was accepted by Herminie's parents as a suitable husband for their daughter. Offenbach and Herminie began what was to be a long and happy marriage on 14 August 1844. Herminie remained at his side throughout, providing a happy family life and

those of Charles Gounod, Offenbach's almost exact contemporary, who became a student there in 1836. He had already obtained his Bachelor of Arts, was a winner of all the prestigious prizes and full of the earnest urge to write masses and grand operas. His first opera, *Sapho,* when it appeared in 1851 was highly praised by Berlioz. Offenbach, however, had no such intentions and dreamed of writing for the theatre.

After only a year's study at the Conservatoire under Cherubini, Jakob departed without distinction, and found himself jobless in the city of Paris. His cello skills helped him to one or two temporary jobs and eventually a regular post in the orchestra at the Opéra-Comique. He also continued to study the cello privately under the well-known cello virtuoso Louis Norblin.

The leading opera composer of the day was Fromental Halévy and Offenbach played in the orchestra for several productions of his operas. Offenbach attended the opening of Halévy's masterpiece *La Juive* as the composer's guest. Halévy was impressed by the enthusiastic young man and gave him some lessons in composing and orchestration. Back at l'Opéra-Comique, he was given more independence and allowed to write some incidental music. He also did some of the hack work for another up-and-coming young composer Friedrich von Flotow and his opera *Martha.*

In the dance-halls the leading names were those of Musard, Tolbecque and Jullien and the young Offenbach, now known as Jacques, was occasionally

Jacques Offenbach was born on 20 June 1819 in Deutz, a suburb of Cologne (above). His natural musical ability found an early outlet in the trio he formed with his brother Julius and sister Isabella. They played in the local dance-halls and cafés, helping considerably to swell the family finances.

Charles Gounod (right), a French composer and Offenbach's exact contemporary, entered the Paris Conservatoire in 1836, but unlike Offenbach was an exemplary student, winning the Grand Prix de Rome in 1839. The success of his opera Faust, first performed in 1859, gave Gounod access to the Opéra, and won him musical respectability.

Musée de l'Opéra. Bulloz

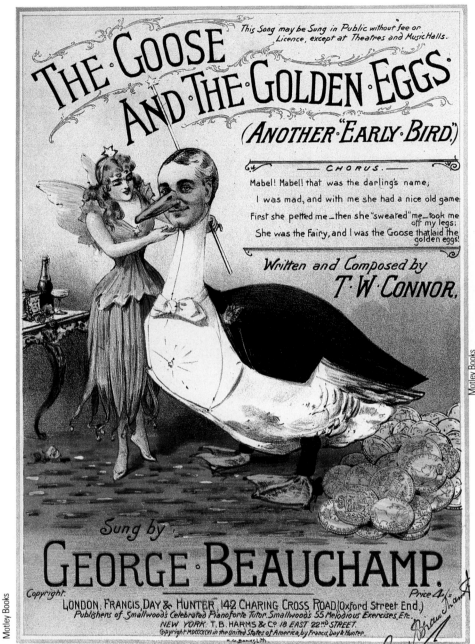

Finding his ambition to compose solely for the established theatre continually thwarted, Offenbach opened a theatre of his own – Les Bouffes-Parisiens. Here he innovated a form of comic opera in which his own sense of humour and brand of music played a central role. An important influence on this came from British music halls which Offenbach visited in London in 1856. The title page (above) of a popular contemporary music hall song gives an idea of the comic nature of these productions.

ignoring his mild flirtations with famous actresses. She was a shadowy but important figure who inspired the tender side of his creations and went on to outlive him by seven years.

The next five or six years saw Offenbach achieve a measure of musical success but as far as his ambitions as a composer went these years proved cruelly frustrating. He was fated to see other composers who had no greater talent than his own becoming more and more famous. When he was commissioned to write operettas there was always something which prevented their production. The final straw came in January 1848 when the revolution of that year stopped the production of an . operetta commissioned by Adolphe Adam for the Théâtre-Lyrique.

Offenbach has been criticized for his actions during this period. He left his Paris house, as he was destined to do again later, during the Franco-Prussian war, and fled with his wife and daughter to Cologne where he changed his name back to Jakob and behaved like a good German, particularly as he

found Cologne itself in revolutionary turmoil. Once the situation in Paris had stabilized Offenbach returned, calling himself Jacques once again, and resumed his crusade to become a writer for the theatre. In 1850 he was offered the job of musical director and conductor at the Comédie Francaise. Here he did much to improve musical standards but tended to quarrel with other members of the company who didn't like the orchestra getting so much attention. However, backed by Arsène Houssaye the director they revitalized the theatre. Although his own compositions found outlet between acts of the main performances his ambition to compose solely for the theatre was continually thwarted.

Working in Paris at the same time was another young operetta composer, Florimond Roger, known by his pen-name of Hervé. Younger than Offenbach, he had solved the problems of finding outlet for his work by founding his own theatre 'Les Folies Nouvelles'. Hervé commissioned a work from Offenbach under the strange title *Oyayaie,* and this had a modest success when produced in June of 1855. Encouraged, Offenbach began to think about founding his own theatre and as it happened that very year proved the turning point for his venture.

Les Bouffes-Parisiens
It was the year of the great Paris International Exhibition and with Paris full of foreign visitors all looking for a good evening's entertainment the time was exactly right for bold new artistic ventures. With a little financial help from his friends, Offenbach took the lease on a very small theatre in the Champs Elysées, called it Les Bouffes-Parisiens and advertised his first production for 5 July 1855. The theatre could only hold an audience of 50 and then only by the use of seats that were so steeply stepped that the audience appeared to be clinging to the rungs of a ladder.

Peter Gammond

PRICE 4/-

The success of Orpheé aux Enfers in 1858 gave Offenbach instant international fame. The scene above is from the first Vienna production in 1860 with the great Johann Nestroy (winged) as Jupiter.

La Périchole (title page above right) was more of a romantic tale and less of a 'normal' Offenbach satire.

Victoria & Albert Museum

Hortense Schneider, the singer (above), as she appeared in the title role of The Grande-Duchesse of Gerolstein. Her admirers included many of the royal visitors (right) to the 1867 Paris world exhibition.

From this point dates the beginning of a fruitful collaboration with a young writer called Ludovic Halévy who wrote the words for the entertainment *Entrez, Messieurs, Mesdames,* which opened Les Bouffes on that historic night. The evening's entertainment included a ballet with Rossini's music arranged by Offenbach and two one-act operettas – one of which *Les Deux Aveugles* (The Two Blind Beggars) became Offenbach's first established piece. The two actors who played the beggars on the first night were so hilariously funny that it made them, the operetta and Les Bouffes-Parisiens famous overnight. Parisiens and foreign visitors heard of this diverting new venue and the demand for the limited number of seats was huge.

Offenbach became an entrepreneur as well as composer and director of the new theatre. The show was such a success it outlived the Paris Exhibition, which had been one of the reasons for starting it, and Offenbach moved the company to a small theatre in the Passage Choiseul for the winter. This was eventually to become the company's permanent home, and Offenbach spent a great deal of time refurbishing it. Meanwhile, Offenbach gave up his conducting job at the Comédie Francaise and began to concentrate on writing.

The first winter season opened on 29 December 1855 with a substantial and effective work called *Ba-ta-clan,* set in a Chinese province where an ex-Parisian rules. The work was highly amusing – Halévy invented a splendid new 'language' for the plot. Even from these early beginnings the pattern for future Offenbach scores, with a mixture of naively sentimental waltzes and vivacious can-cans, was clearly discernible. Offenbach was aware that he was creating a new – more national – genre, and therefore playing a part in forming an original style, rather than simply bowing to or borrowing from the established Italian style of opera that was prevalent at the time. He also realised his ambition of reviving the tradition of opéra-comique. In the early days of the Bouffes-Parisiens Offenbach auditioned the young Hortense Schneider. She was an instant success in *Le Violoneux* in August 1855 and during the next 12 years starred in most of Offenbach's major operettas.

In 1856 Offenbach and his directors announced a competition. The prize offered was 1200 francs and a medal for a one-act operetta in the style set by Les Bouffes. The panel of distinguished judges included Auber, Halévy, Thomas, Scribe and Charles Gounod, the latter a respected member of the musical establishment (but who had yet to write his greatest masterpiece, *Faust*). An eliminating test produced six candidates from a field of 18 entrants. They were asked to set to music a libretto called *Le Docteur Miracle* written by Halévy and Leon Battu. The result was a draw between Lecocq and Georges Bizet – two composers set for distinction at a later date.

For the new summer season, Les Bouffes-Parisiens moved back again to the Champs Elysées and continued to thrive. After this it moved back,

Roger Viollet

permanently, to the theatre in the Passage Choiseul.

In London in 1857 he was welcomed back as conductor and composer rather than as the virtuoso cellist he had been on his first visit. The season was organized by a relative of Offenbach's parents-in-law, John Mitchell, and the season was so successful that Offenbach sent for the rest of the company in order to extend it further.

Wealth and fame

Back home in Paris the family finances were in such a good state that they were able to move to a very respectable house in the Rue Lafitte, near the Rothschilds. This house became the hectic musical centre with Friday evening parties attended by Bizet, Delibes and Gustave Doré.

Offenbach's lavish hospitality at home and the generous amount of money he spent on his theatre, always keeping it spick and span, put pressure on him to produce new and greater productions. So in 1858

Offenbach's rather eccentric appearance was caricatured to great effect by cartoonists of the day. In the cartoon by Gill (below) – drawn for the cover of a satirical magazine – he is shown astride his cello, surrounded by characters from his operettas.

The Villa Orphée (above), the holiday home built for the family in Normandy, was paid for from the proceeds of Orphée aux Enfers.

Michel Brindejont

he embarked on his first substantial show. The archaic licencing laws which had only allowed him a small cast of four were lifted and the way was open for as lavish a production as the small theatre would allow. The amusing account of the frantic behind-the-scenes activity at Les Bouffes Parisien in the Paris magazine, *Journal Amusant,* gives us a glimpse into the chaotic way Offenbach and his company worked. This describes the general scene of the first day of production of *Orphée aux Enfers* (Orpheus in the Underworld) where there were actors demanding new costumes, friends asking for free seats, a shortage of musicians, the bailiffs arriving and having to be pacified, a burst gas main, and a list of cuts from the censor.

Orphée was a hard-hitting lampoon, on one level of a classical story, on another, of classical music. Many critics were deeply offended at Offenbach's irreverent use of Gluck's works, but most found it a sharp satire which they secretly enjoyed but publicly deplored as bad taste. People were a little dubious about being seen there and business was slow. Possibly the show would have won through on its own eventually because of its splendid music but matters were brought to a head by an all-out attack launched by a prominent critic, Jules Janin, who was deeply shocked and found it 'a profanation of holy and glorious antiquity'. This, however, proved to be its making – the very suggestion of something shocking did the trick. The demand for seats grew overwhelmingly and it seemed that all Paris wanted to see and talk about *Orphée*. Above all the new brand of music that Offenbach had to offer was now able to show itself to the full and his works found their way abroad where they influenced composers in Vienna, London and New York.

In 1860 the Bouffes Parisien was accorded the honour of an entry in small book in a series of guides to the Paris theatres – a signal of acceptance. At last

Peter Gammond

In 1876, due to a variety of circumstances, Offenbach found himself in financial difficulties. Consequently, although he was in poor health, he was tempted by the offer of $30,000 to conduct a concert tour of America. The tour, celebrating the Centenary of the Declaration of Independence, was a great success. On his return to France Offenbach wrote an account of his journey, Orpheus in America. *The English edition of 1876 (cover, left) was entitled* America and the Americans.

related to his intake of good food and wine.

The theatre housing Les Bouffes Parisiens was rebuilt to accommodate larger audiences and in 1864 it saw a triumph in the same league as *Orphée – La Belle Hélène.* Although *La Belle Hélène* attracted large audiences, the critics felt it was another desecration of antiquity. Nevertheless, the ensuing years were fruitful – *Barbe-Bleue* (Bluebeard) appeared in 1866, followed by the most scintillating of all his works *La Vie Parisienne* which evokes the sophisticated spirit of the Paris which everyone imagines. Next, and coinciding with the great Paris World Exhibition of 1867, came the greatest international success – *La Grande-Duchesse de Gérolstein.* Hortense Schneider was so supreme in this role that she acted her part of the Grande-Duchesse off-stage as well as on-stage.

The last years

There were a few halting steps in Offenbach's success though. *La Périchole,* for example, his most romantic operetta, was not quite scandalous enough to be a major success despite containing one of Offenbach's finest arias, the famous Letter Song, which Hortense Schneider put over with artful simplicity. And the Franco-Prussian war appears to have cut the flow of his inspiration in 1870 and for most of 1871, but by now his operettas were flourishing abroad. *The Princess of Trebizonde* opened in London in 1870 and Offenbach went over to see the production.

Offenbach's work reached l'Opéra – a ballet, *Le Papillon* choreographed by the great Taglioni and featuring a new star Emma Livry. It was an enormous success at the time and although the ballet unaccountably disappeared from the repertoire, until revived in modern times, its main tune, the 'Valse de Rayons' lived on as one of Offenbach's best known melodies. By 1862 the bad health that was to plague Offenbach's later years began to show itself. Some of the symptoms were due to overwork but the severe attacks of gout he suffered were directly

Offenbach's lasting contribution to French popular music of the 19th century was his restoration of the Gallic traditions of wit and vivacity in the Opéra-Comique (below), when it was in danger of being swamped by Italian influences.

Offenbach retreated from Paris as the Republic was declared and his work, denounced as 'Prussian' because of his German origins, immediately went out of favour. Lecocq, a jealous rival, declared that the reign of Offenbach was no more popular abroad than in his own country. In response Offenbach re-wrote many of his operettas for the Théâtre de la Gâité, but they were often over-inflated and not so popular. He suffered some financial losses with this series of works and was forced into bankruptcy. With his fortunes so low, Offenbach felt obliged to restore them by accepting with reluctance (for he was unwell) an invitation to visit America for the World Exhibition in Philadelphia. The Americans obviously expected a wicked Parisian figure who would dance the can-can on the platform. Instead he cut a small, forlorn and rather serious figure, homesick for his family and France. His concerts in Philadelphia were well-attended, and his music became established in America.

Back in France, Offenbach continued to write – *Madame Favart* produced in 1878 was a pleasant *succes d'estime* at l'Opéra Comique, the old fortress he had so often tried to storm. From 1877 onwards Offenbach had been obsessed with a desire to write a Grand Opera and as his theme settled on some of the fantastic *Tales of Hoffman.* On this work, thin and tired, he toiled away in what was to be his last year of life. Sadly there were endless delays in the progress of the production of this, but in the meantime he managed one more first-rate operetta – La Fille du Tambour Major. Finally, in September 1880, he was able to attend a rehearsal of 'The Tales' and in October he played the score through to the cast.

The next day he had a choking fit and lapsed into recurrent bouts of unconsciousness. On the morning of 5 October 1880 he died of gout of the heart. An old comedian friend called to see him and was told by Monsieur Leonce, the porter: 'Monsieur Offenbach died without knowing it.' 'He will be surprised when he finds out!'

Roger Viollet

Gaieté Parisienne
Faust – Ballet music

Two very different sides of the musical scene of late 19th-century France clearly emerge in these works from Jacques Offenbach and Charles Gounod.

Gaieté Parisienne

For almost 20 years, from 1855 onwards, Jacques Offenbach was the hero of the Parisian scene. His vivacious, exuberant music, with its lashings of satirical wit, seemed the very spirit of 'Gay Paree' – the street cafés, the Bouffes-Parisiens and the Moulin Rouge. And Parisians, always attracted to lively, Bohemian sensuality, lapped up such pieces as *Orpheus in the Underworld* and *La Grand-Duchesse de Gerolstein*. Despite this, Offenbach's work proved to be very much music of its time, and eventually his popularity evaporated like the bubbles in a glass of champagne – enjoyed but soon forgotten.

Then, in 1932, the Ballets Russes de Monte Carlo emerged to carry on the Diaghilev Ballets Russes tradition and began the search for new ballet material. By 1937 Leonide Massine, the principal dancer and choreographer with the Ballets

Russes de Serge Diaghilev, joined the new company and with an American tour in mind, both he and the Ballets Russes' director, Réné Blum, felt that new works of a lighter nature were needed. The idea of a ballet set in Paris in the splendid, frivolous and rather naughty period of the Second Empire immediately suggested the music of Offenbach. And his operetta, *La Vie Parisienne* of 1866 which had been such a wonderful evocation of these times, capturing a light-hearted world of gaiety, unscrupulousness and artificiality, seemed to fit the bill perfectly. The Ballets Russes therefore put together a glorious compilation of his work, based largely on this operetta, called it *Gaieté Parisienne,* and staged it as a ballet. Offenbach's music, in modified form, was popular once more.

La Vie Parisienne had been a satire on the Paris of Offenbach's day, parodying contemporary characters and the social scene with the composer's characteristic

wit and panache. But with his usual commercial sense, Offenbach set the action on the boulevards, so that he could bring tourists into the plot – thus ensuring that both Parisians and foreigners would have characters to identify with. When it was first performed in the Palais-Royal in Paris, the Parisians loved it. Abroad however, it was less successful. Perhaps the main reason for this was because it was so very Parisian – the very ingredient that was to be the strength of the Ballets Russes' *Gaieté Parisienne.*

Making of the ballet

The plot for the ballet was devised by the artistic director and designer Comte Etienne de Beaumont and the choreographer Massine, and it was originally to be titled Tortoni, after the famous café of Offenbach's time in the Boulevard des Italiens. De Beaumont and Massine did not need to look much further than *La Vie*

One of the major tourist attractions of 19th-century Paris was the Folies Bergère (right). Only three years after Offenbach's success with La Vie Parisienne *this famous music hall opened its doors to an excited public. The entertainments were lavish and included vaudeville sketches, operettas, eccentric dancers, magicians and the like – capturing the very essence of 'Gay Paree'.*

Soldiers returning from Algeria introduced the Can-Can (right) to Paris in the 1830s. The dance became immensely popular especially after Offenbach's inclusion of it in his operetta Orphée aux Enfers. *Despite protests from puritan elements of society, nothing could stop the ladies of Paris kicking their legs high in the air, showing their garters and titillating audiences with this 'naughty' dance.*

Parisienne for material and the third act of that work more or less provided the action and the setting of the ballet. The character of the Glove Seller, the Peruvian (originally a Brazilian), the Baron and an Officer also came from the third act.

The orchestrations were arranged by the composer and conductor, Manuel Rosenthal. With the guidance of Offenbach's nephew, Jacques Brindejont-Offenbach, Rosenthal chose musical excerpts mainly from *La Vie Parisienne,* but included also sections from *Orpheus in the Underworld, La Belle Hélène, La Perichole* and *Tales of Hoffman* among the better-known works; and from lesser-known pieces he used *Mesdames de la Halle, Le Voyage dans la Lune, Lischen et Fritzchen* and *Tromb-al-Cazar.* For a few sections, such as the duel, Rosenthal wrote some passages of original music. But for the most part Offenbach's own orchestrations fitted the bill perfectly — being both witty and colourful — and all that was needed was to fill them out a little. Some critics disapproved at the time, as Massine did, and Rosenthal's orchestrations were described as brash. In fact, Rosenthal himself has told

of how the score, on completion, was turned down by Massine who thought that not enough respect had been accorded to Offenbach's music. Rosenthal suggested that a second opinion should be sought and made the rather strange choice of Stravinsky, whose *Rite of Spring* Rosenthal had conducted in 1937. Stravinsky, of course, was an experienced writer of ballets for Diaghilev but one would hardly think of him as an Offenbach admirer. Yet, after hearing the score Stravinsky told Massine with some force that it would be idiotic to reject it for it might well be the greatest success the company had had for some time. Stravinsky had lived in Paris for many years and appreciated just how vividly Offenbach's music evoked the friviolous social life of the city.

The score

Far from being brash, Rosenthal's orchestrations now seem admirably crisp, and tasteful in showing a natural affinity with the originals — and are compiled with the hand of a first-class and clever craftsman.

The original overture to the operetta was, as is so often the case with overtures, a

The fashionable Café Tortoni on the Boulevard des Italiens (above) provided the setting (and the original title) for Gaieté Parisienne.

restrained piece, and Rosanthal modified this to a hilarious romp for 'Gaieté'. But this matches the tone of the work as a whole and therefore fits in happily.

Looking through the *Lia Vie Parisienne* score with a discerning eye Rosenthal then drew from it a lively Mazurka, a secondary waltz theme and its lively Can-Can, which rivals the more famous one from *Orpheus* for sheer verve and tunefulness. But most importantly, he took two themes that hold much of the essence of Offenbach's Paris in their melodies: Metella's (the female lead in the opera) waltz-theme from Act IV 'A minuit sonnant commence la fête' — which is a waltz that only Offenbach could have written; and the Peruvian's (Brazilian in the opera) song from Act 1, again totally Offenbach in its feel.

Having raided this work for its gems, Rosenthal then turned to Offenbach's first great major success *Orpheus in the Underworld* which set Les Bouffes Parisiens on its feet in 1858. From it he took the truly splendid waltz which Orpheus plays on his violin in the famous Concerto scene of Act 1, a bubbling polka and inevitably the famous Can-Can which is one of the opera's chief glories – simple yet so theatrically effective. From *La Belle Hélène* (1864) came an elegant polka, and, from Offenbach's 'grand' swan-song *The Tales of Hoffman,* a fine waltz from the first story and the unavoidable Barcarolle which provides the dramatically quiet ending to the ballet. From *La Perichole* (1868), the light story of two young lovers involved in the political machinations of Peru, Rosenthal took the most moving of all Offenbach melodies, the famous Letter Song.

For the rest of the 'Gaieté' scene, he found some of those striking themes from lesser-known one-act pieces.

World-wide success

Finally titled *Gaieté Parisienne,* the ballet had its first performance at the Théâtre de Monte Carlo on April 5, 1938 where it was enthusiastically received. The leading dancers were Nina Tarakanova as the Glove Seller, Leonide Massine as the Peruvian, Eugenie Delarova as the Flower Girl, Jeanette Lauret as La Lionne, Igor Youskevitch as the Officer and Frederick Franklin as the Baron. The part of the Glove Seller was later taken over by Alexandra Danilova who made it one of her most successful roles.

Within the year the company had taken the ballet to New York and London where it found equal popularity.

There is a tendency to use such words as frothy and frivolous in connection with Offenbach's music, yet this ballet has had unfailing success to this day. This demonstrates the usual highbrow tendency to underestimate anything which has obvious and sometimes simple attractions. But the music is, in fact, a remarkably sustained exercise in vivacity on the one hand and grace and charm on the other; and in spite of its lightness, it has a great and lasting strength.

Programme notes

After a rumbustious overture, underlaid with plenty of percussion, which whirls us into the action of the ballet, the curtain rises on the Café Tortoni, the fashionable Paris restaurant with its marble-topped tables, gilt chairs and chandeliers. It is mid-19th century, the time of the Second Empire. The waiters and waitresses are preparing the tables and the boys amuse the girls with an athletic and comic polka. To the rhythmic strains of the Landler the Flower-Girl enters, much admired by the

The Ballets Russes de Monte Carlo's **Gaieté Parisienne** *(right) was a sparkling ballet set to a glorious compilation of Offenbach's melodies. The costumes (below) were designed by Comte Etienne de Beaumont.*

The souvenir programme of the Ballets Russes season in London (far right).

Understanding music: light classical music

Many wonder how they can arrive at an appreciation of great music without having to study it in great depth or learn its history. But there is an easy and enjoyable way: simply by listening to what one finds most immediately approachable, a greater appetite for more demanding music, and a better understanding of it, are quickly acquired. This, then, is the purpose and essence of what is termed 'light classical' music – music that is approachable, immediately enjoyable and which can provide a link to understanding more involved works.

The art of writing good light music is a very special one, and one that great composers find just as elusive as lesser composers. 'Unfortunately not by me' wrote Brahms under a quotation from *The Blue Danube*. Yet Brahms himself, a heavyweight composer in more ways than one, was capable of writing music that was light, attractive and undemanding – as in his piano waltzes and vivacious Hungarian dances. While Mozart put most effort into his unmatched series of great piano concertos, he also wrote quite simple, straightforward serenades and divertimentos for the noble, but not necessarily intellectual, patrons who paid him. After they had dined to the serenade, Mozart supplied his lords and ladies with plenty of light-hearted dances; as did Schubert, later, for his patrons and friends. If music is to be danced to, it must remain uncomplicated. Thus, a century further on, we find some of the most popular and approachable light music of all time in the ballets that Tchaikovsky wrote.

There is hardly a great composer who has not found time to write at least one light classic and, because they were great composers who wrote everything in a dedicated way, the light pieces are usually true samples of their more profound music. For example, Sibelius's *Valse triste,* part of the incidental music he wrote for the play *Kuolema,* revolves around a central character sitting at the bedside of his dying mother. Hardly a 'light' theme, yet the music is light and charming but with all of Sibelius's substance and strength.

An interesting example of a composer who wrote in all spheres with the same unaffected ease was Sir Edward Elgar (1857–1934). On the one hand, his symphonies, concertos and oratorios were long and demanding works. On the other hand, the light touch, when asked for, was assured and uncondescending as in such pieces as *Salut d'amour, Chanson de matin,* the *Pomp and Circumstance* marches, and the delightful music he wrote for a play called *The Starlight Express.*

If the great masters have their lighter moments, there are also those composers who were masters of the craft of writing light music. No composer, however prestigious, has challenged the younger Johann Strauss (pages 33-51). Many of his waltzes manage to be substantial concert pieces as well as dances, with elaborate atmospheric introductions and cleverly balanced juxtapositions of themes. Strauss's operetta, *Die Fledermaus,* insistently, almost extravagantly, tuneful throughout, has a perfection and craft that few grand operas can challenge.

A prolific craftsman, Offenbach wrote over 100 operettas and there is hardly one that does not contain some gem. The British equivalent of these two masters was Sir Arthur Sullivan (1842–1900). Showing himself a total master of light music in the operettas he wrote with W. S. Gilbert, Sullivan, nonetheless, had another side – as the serious composer of oratorios and symphonies. Fine as these heavier works are, he remains a master of light music, the best example being his *Di Ballo* overture which has a bit of both worlds in its zestful balletic themes.

It is thus a small step from such light music to the weightier delights of Haydn's *'Surprise',* Mozart's *'Jupiter'* or Beethoven's *'Pastoral'* Symphonies – all of them involved works where lightness reigns supreme. So, if longer works seem daunting it is good to approach them through shorter ones, just as one jogs a little before joining a marathon.

Tuneful gems from the classics have always been adapted for popular use.

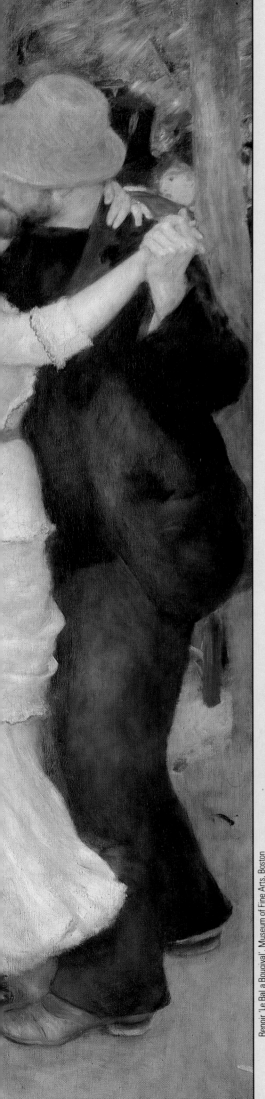

Renoir 'Le Bal a Bougival': Museum of Fine Arts, Boston

waiters. She presents each boy with a bouquet and is given a glass of champagne. The Flower Girl drinks a toast to her waiter friends and together they dance. A group of Cocodettes ('flirtatious girls of loose character') enter with their male escorts. The girls are flashily dressed, the men wear the typical Parisian black jackets and berets. While the Flower Girl sets up her stand, the Cocodettes and their friends dance a lively Mazurka. The charming and beautiful Glove Seller (immediately surrounded by all the men) enters to the strains of Metella's Waltz:

Example 1

She is only anxious to sell her gloves but the men insist on dancing with her first.

There is a distraction now in the shape of a bustling, dandyish little foreigner from Peru on holiday in Paris:

Example 2

He has plenty of money to spend on the ladies of the town and intends to enjoy his night out. So eager is he to start his fun that he is still carrying his luggage which he drops as he sees the Flower Girl who places

The waltz tunes that are so much a part of 'Gaieté's' charm are very definitely Parisian rather than Viennese in feel and are every bit as lilting and graceful as any by Johann Strauss. Many of the most famous waltzes were taken from Offenbach's La Vie Parisienne *(below).*

LAUROS/Giraudon

a flower in his button hole. The only person who ignores his advances is the Glove Seller, which makes him, of course, all the more fascinated by her. He purchases a pair of gloves from her which she tries to put on his hands while he still dances about in his excitement. The handsome Baron enters to the family waltz from Orpheus. A waiter takes his cape revealing his immaculate dress which catches the attention of the girls. But he ignores the others and goes to the Glove Seller whom he courteously invites to join him in a dance to the romantic waltz-strains.

Meanwhile, the Peruvian is having a good time with the Cocodettes. He orders champagne but it is not to his expensive taste. He orders another with which he is satisfied and pours a glass for each of the ladies. Suddenly, everyone's pleasure is interrupted by the arrival of a group of soldiers and an Officer who arrogantly expect the girls to focus all attention on them. They perform a military dance with mock shooting and drill, and the girls pretend to send them off to war. Into the restaurant now comes La Lionne, known as the Toast of Paris. She greets the assembled company flaunting a red velvet dress which infuriates the other girls but fascinates the men. Her escort, an elderly Duke, is slightly embarrassed by her. La Lionne sets her sights on the Officer who is thus seduced away from the Glove Seller with whom he has had no success. The Peruvian, having been snubbed by La Lionne, now attempts to kiss the Glove Seller. The Baron is infuriated and attacks the Officer, and soon there is a discordant free-for-all in progress. The Peruvian hides in terror under a table. When quiet is finally restored he rushes out carrying the table on his head.

In the end the Baron and the Glove Seller are reconciled and dance a romantic waltz together to the tune of the Letter Song:

Example 3

After this the restaurant resumes its normal entertaining activities. The saucy Can-Can dancers whirl in led by a male dancer and dance their exotic showpiece ending in the athletic splits. Everyone now joins in a hectic dance. The Peruvian, returning in top hat, is spun round and round by the dancing girls and the dance whirls on to an exuberant climax to the evening. The lights are lowered, the ladies find their cloaks and the couples vanish into the night to the quiet swaying strains of the Barcarolle. The Baron partnered by the Glove Seller, the Flower Girl with the Duke, La Lionne with the Officer, depart, waving goodbye to the Peruvian. We hear a little echoing snatch of his theme. He is left sadly holding his suitcase as the music comes to a close.

Faust

While Offenbach frantically pursued his career of popular composer and impresario, Charles Gounod, his contemporary, was treading the path of respectability in the more serious musical world. Born just one year earlier than Offenbach on 18 June 1818, Gounod was a genuine 'French' Parisian. He had a classical education and was a Bachelor of Arts before he entered the Paris Conservatoire in 1836.

During a relatively promising career, he wrote his first opera, *Sapho,* in 1851. It was highly praised by Berlioz and quickly established Gounod as a recognized composer – in contrast to Offenbach's continual struggles for acceptance. But it was *Faust,* produced in 1859, that eventually made Gounod a successful opera composer. The first performance on 19 March was attended by an audience that included many distinguished composers and critics. Most of the latter were rather lukewarm in their comments. One who had criticized

Sapho previously for its lack of melody found the same fault in Faust. The one person who praised it was again Berlioz – generous from one who had written *La Damnation de Faust* and had seen it fail way back in 1846. But experts aside, the public loved *Faust* and it was performed at the Théâtre-Lyrique 57 times before the end of 1859.

After many productions abroad, *Faust* arrived at l'Opéra in Paris, in 1869. In those days the l'Opéra supported a large ballet company and every opera produced there was expected to make use of this facility. It was at this stage that Gounod dutifully added the now well-known ballet music as described in this chapter. *Faust* did a great deal for French grand opera, establishing a new romantic tradition just as the opera comique style seemed to be

losing popularity and Offenbach was branching out in lighter directions.

The Faust story, based on Goethe's epic drama, tells how Faust, failing in old age, calls upon the Devil to aid him. Mephistopheles, the Devil's agent, offers wealth and power, but in return wants Faust's soul. Spurred by a vision of the fair Marguerite, Faust agrees. Valentine, Marguerite's brother is off to the wars and is concerned for her safety. Mephistopheles taunts Valentine and his friend Siebel who is in love with Marguerite and, in accordance with his pact, brings her and Faust together. In her garden, Siebel tries to pick flowers for Marguerite but they wilt in his hands. Marguerite finally falls in love with Faust much to the Devil's sardonic amusement. Valentine, returning from the wars, challenges Faust to a duel. Mephistopheles intervenes and Valentine is killed. Faust has a sudden vision of Marguerite and demands to see her. But she is in prison, condemned for the murder of her child, and going mad. She dies and the angels take her soul. Faust is dragged away to eternal damnation.

Faust – the ballet

When Gounod was told to add a ballet to this he must have faced a considerable problem. But he cleverly solved the matter by going outside the tragic love story of Faust and Marguerite and drawing on the second part of Goethe's epic which features the legendary revels said to have

A poster advertising a production of Faust *at the Academie Nationale de Musique (left). It was the success of* Faust *that brought Gounod recognition as an opera composer and fame to Marie Miolan-Carvalho (below) as a singer.*

The story of Faust – the man who sold his soul to the devil (above) – has long been a source of inspiration and fascination in the world of music, art and literature.

taken place on Walpurgis Night (the evening before May Day) on Brocken, the highest peak of the Hartz mountains.

The ballet does not tell a story as such, as it is in the then-popular form of a *divertimento,* a series of character dances that so often appear as the finale to the classical ballets. In Gounod's approach, these dances centre on Faust's introduction, by the Devil, to some of the ladies of antiquity, mostly with somewhat infamous reputations. Faust is then transported to a region of Will-o'-the-Wisps, Witches and Wizards that dwell in Mephistopheles' domain in the mountains. The side of the mountain opens to reveal a great palace, shining with gold. In the middle there is a table, richly spread: around it are seated the queens and courtesans of antiquity. After drinking with them Faust is entertained by their dances.

Programme notes

Gounod wrote a new score for the ballet but kept the link with the opera by using vague echoes of the previous work's main melodies in distorted versions.

In the ballet score the movements are only identified by tempo markings and the corresponding action in the ballet is as follows. Aspasia and Lais, leaders of the courtesans, invite Faust and Mephistopheles to join their feast *(Allegretto Mouvement de Valse)*. Cleopatra and her Nubian slave girls *(Adagio)* and Helen of Troy with her attendants *(Allegretto)* surround Faust in a seductive way. The Nubian slaves drink Cleopatra's poisoned draught from golden cups, and she takes a sip herself from a goblet in which she has dissolved her most precious jewels *(Variations of Cleopatra: Moderato maestoso)*. The Trojan women with Helen of Troy now dance *(Moderato con moto)*; and then Venus's rival Astarte is seen at her mirror *(Mirror variations: Allegretto)* – a melody which could have come straight out of an operetta:

Example 4

All these seductive scenes are quelled for a moment by the arrival of Phryne, wrapped in a veil. She lets the veil fall, stands revealed and urges the dance on until it become a wild orgy *(Allegro vivo)*.

At this point, Faust sees an apparition of Marguerite, flings his goblet away, and the palace with all its weird inmates suddenly vanishes as the ballet closes.

Great interpreters

Orchestra of the Royal Opera House

Remarkably, before World War II Covent Garden had no permanently chartered house ensemble or company: only gifted individuals and powerful personalities, such as Sir Thomas Beecham, provided the funding, organization and the orchestras which made it possible to mount each successive season of productions. This all changed in the aftermath of the War when Boosey and Hawkes took out a long-term lease on the theatre and allowed it to be re-established as an opera and ballet house with a permanently organized company which had government support.

Under the general administrator, David Webster, the newly formed Covent Garden Opera Company was slowly built up into a world-class organization with a tradition of its own.

Three musical directors helped immensely in the efforts to upgrade and maintain the musical standards of the company, often against the odds and in the face of biting criticism: Karl Rankl (1946–51), Rafael Kubelik (1955–8) and Georg Solti (1961–71). Under Solti, in particular, the orchestra was honed to a very high standard and the repertoire was broadened, helping to make the Opera House one of the best in the world again. In 1968 the Opera House Company became the Royal Opera by consent of Queen Elizabeth, and has remained so ever since.

Under Sir Colin Davis (1971-87) the musical standards have been maintained both in the orchestra pit and on the stage. Since 1987, Bernard Haitink has continued to pursue a vigorous musical policy.

FURTHER LISTENING

Orpheus in the Underworld
This racy and entertaining satire on both Gluck and the old legend which Gluck had used for his greatest opera was looked upon as both scandalous and shocking when it was premiered in Paris. To present a Eurydice who is bored with Orpheus and flirting with three other men, and an Orpheus who is distinctly reluctant to rescue his wife from Hades, seemed at the time a savage attack on convention. The inclusion of the famous Can-Can, which some considered risqué, was also provocative. Today, of course, such things have ceased to titillate, and it is the sheer verve of the music and the libretto which continue to keep this operetta before the public.

La Belle Hélène
This was the second wildly successful updating by Offenbach of old mythical subjects. Using the same procedure as in Orpheus, he and his librettists concentrated on the successful abduction of Helen by the Trojan Paris. Here the Greeks are the figures of ridicule, with Achilles, for example, constantly bothered by a sore heel. Today, even after most of the contemporary references to the satire have faded, the inspired melodies, the genuinely funny action and the gusto of the music combine successfully.

The Tales of Hoffman
Offenbach's last opera, based on the fantastic tales of ETA Hoffman, was intended to be his crowning achievement. He wrote it as a sick man and with the knowledge of approaching death. It is a serious work, far removed from his earlier satires and farces, and it is clear that Offenbach was committed to at last writing a work in the grand opera tradition. The task was unfinished at his death, though all the essentials had been completed, and when a collaborator put the finishing touches on it it was recognized as one of the greatest operas of the age.

IN THE BACKGROUND

'War to the knife'

***With the strains of Offenbach's music still ringing
in the streets, Paris prepared for battle with
Prussia. Offenbach escaped, but Parisians went
on through the bloodiest phase in their history.***

Bildarchiv Preussischer Kulturbesitz

Roger Viollet

*The two main
protagonists in the
Franco-Prussian War
of 1870–1871, Otto von
Bismarck (above) and
Napoleon III (above
right). Napoleon's
vainglorious notion of
stemming the growing
might of Prussia led the
French, and Parisians
in particular, into
dark days of defeat
and civil strife.*

When France took the decision to go to war against
Prussia on 19 July 1870, an easy victory was confidently expected. Within one week such illusions
were shattered as early defeats left France's eastern
provinces of Alsace and Lorraine open to invasion. In
declaring war, France had unleashed a catastrophic
train of events which in less than a year would swell
the pages of history. Between July 1870 and May
1871 France saw the end of the Second Empire, the
establishment of a republic and a humiliating
military defeat. She suffered a Draconian peace
settlement and a siege of her capital on two
occasions: first by Prussian troops and secondly,
following the outbreak of civil war, by troops of the
new French Republic. The two sieges make interesting comparison: the defence of the city against

Prussia was a heroic but futile struggle, while the
second was a tragic episode. Of the second siege, *The
Times* wrote, 'The French are filling up the darkest
page in the book of their or the World's history.'

The road to war

Just as the groundswell of nationalism in Italy in the
1850s saw the creation of a united state, so the 1860s
witnessed the rapid development of German national
feeling. The decade was punctuated by wars of
unification fought against Denmark and Austria.
Following victory in this latter conflict, the growing
strength of Prussia presented a serious challenge to
the European balance of power and to French
security. Gripped by an outburst of patriotism,
French public opinion feared that Bismarck (the

Prussian Chancellor) would unite Germany by merging the southern states into the Prussian dominated North German Confederation. Many felt that to allow this would be an irrevocable abdication of France's greatness. The feeling grew that war between France and Prussia was inevitable: this feeling precipitated events in 1870.

Since Prussia's swift defeat of Austria in 1866, the French emperor Napoleon III had sought allies against this new German might — or instead, territorial compensation. In the first he failed, as French adventures in Italy and Mexico had alarmed countries like Britain, an alarm deepened by Napoleon's suggestion to Bismark that France should be ceded Belgium. His other demand — for part of the Rhineland — angered all Germany.

French ministerial and public opinion was infuriated when the Prussian royal family, the

abridged version of the telegram to the press in the hope of provoking France into an ill-considered response. Bismarck's version suggested an acrimonious exchange had taken place between William and Benedetti. Outraged French public opinion demanded war. By prolonging the affair the French had played into the hand of Bismarck, who had succeeded in goading France into a war which he calculated would enable him to put the finishing touches to German unification. But the responsibilty for war was not all Bismarck's. French ministers did nothing to pacify public opinion and there was plainly a lack of calm and balance on their part. They had made a false move in pressing for a guarantee and feared to draw back, being swept along by a floodtide of partisan sentiment.

Preparations for siege

Despite her optimism, France was in no state to fight a major war. She could only muster a force of 350,000, she underestimated the power of the Prussian army and failed to appreciate the importance of artillery. The French forces were outmanoeuvred by the better-commanded Prussians. Paris was stunned by this string of early setbacks, especially as rumours had been rife that the army of the Crown Prince of Prussia had been captured. (The rumour had started in a successful attempt to rig the Stock Exchange.) Reluctantly, the city prepared for siege as the

The Ems Telegram (left) which sparked the conflict. The original was sent by Kaiser William I of Prussia to his Chancellor, Bismarck, informing him of a diplomatic exchange between himself and the French Ambassador to Berlin, Benedetti.

Bildarchiv Preussischer Kulturbesitz

Bulloz

Hohenzollerns, nominated a candidate for the vacant Spanish throne. France regarded Spain as her own sphere of influence and was appalled by the prospect of Leopold von Hohenzollern ruling Spain. Benedetti, the French ambassador to Berlin, however, successfully persuaded Kaiser William I to withdraw the nomination. (The idea had been Bismarck's, and William was not enthusiastic about it.) But instead of accepting William's word, the French were driven on by bellicose opinion at home and disastrously overplayed their hand. They demanded a formal guarantee that the candidacy would never again be renewed. William refused and, from the holiday spa of Ems, sent a telegram to Bismarck informing him of his intentions. On receiving the communication, Bismarck took the initiative — he released an

prospect was hard to grasp. Paris saw itself as the centre of civilization — the cosmopolitan capital of the world. As recently as 1867, the city played host to hundreds of thousands of visitors who flocked to the city to visit the Universal Exhibition, to admire the marvellous boulevards of Baron Haussmann, and to watch Napoleon III's splendid military parade in the Bois de Boulogne. Entertainers and whores flocked to the Exhibition — Paris was not only the centre of culture, but of fun as well. Opera and ballet flourished. Visitors were regaled with the music of Offenbach, and Strauss — never one to miss an occasion — contributed a new waltz, *The Blue Danube*. What a contrast, then, in that September as over 3000 heavy cannon were brought to the city, transforming Paris from a city of pleasure to a

Paris prepares for siege (above) in the early days of the war, transforming itself from a city of pleasure, gaiety and music into a massive fortress. Here, troops are shown encamped in the gardens of the Tuileries.

The war went badly for France from the start and the French army soon found itself besieged at Metz. In her capacity as Regent, Napoleon's wife, Empress Eugenie (right), ordered the last remaining strong force, under General MacMahon, to relieve the army trapped at Metz. Her decision was disastrous, as the ensuing Battle of Sedan proved.

massive fortress. A quarter of a million sheep were brought into the Luxembourg Gardens, and 40,000 oxen put out to pasture inside the city walls. But the authorities did not expect the siege to last into winter. Stocks of flour and coal were insufficient, and so too was the provision of dairy stock.

The war continued to go badly for France. By late August the largest French force of 173,000 under General Bazaine was pinned down at the eastern town of Metz. The only notable army remaining was at Châlons under the command of MacMahon. This catalogue of defeats left the feeling in Paris that the end of Napoleon's empire was nigh. The Governor of Paris, General Trochu, insisted that Napoleon – fighting alongside MacMahon – return to Paris. The

Empress Eugenie, however, feared for her husband's life. With the authority of Regent, she instructed MacMahon to relieve the French army besieged at Metz. The decision was foolhardy – she had sent MacMahon, her husband and an army of 84,000 to their capture, at the ensuing Battle of Sedan. No disaster in French history was more complete or humiliating.

Political consequences soon followed: in a bloodless coup on 4 September, the Second French Empire was overthrown. The Empress fled to London, to be joined by Napoleon the following year. The Emperor died in 1873, a broken man.

The siege begins

Soon after Sedan the Prussians arrived outside the gates of Paris – the first siege was about to begin. Despite the increasing hopelessness of the military situation, nationalistic pride, together with enthusiasm at the prospect of establishing a radical republic, made Parisians eager to continue the fight. Parallels were drawn with a similar situation during the great French Revolution. Then, faced with an invading foreign army, France was saved by her people. Though the new Government of National Defence consisted mainly of conservatives, uncertain about carrying the fight to Prussia, it was driven on by ardent Republicans, such as Gambetta and Rochefort who dreamt of a *levée en masse* (conscription) which would stem the tide. The Prussians, however, were similarly determined. Bismarck felt that victory with substantial territorial gains would make German unity irresistible. There could be no compromise – it was 'war to the knife'.

Only a fortnight into the siege the food supply was seen to be dwindling. Although the only problem for the wealthy was whether their diet had been adulterated with horse flesh, the poor found meat difficult to find at all. Some were reduced to raiding the drains for rats. Butchers refused to sell at prices fixed by the government, which provoked violent scenes. People began waiting in line at 2am in the hope of getting provisions. Bread was still plentiful, but eggs, vegetables and fish were scarce and greatly over-priced.

In the catalogue of disasters and defeats that make up the pages of French history in the war, the Battle of Sedan (right) ranks as the most catastrophic. Napoleon, along with General MacMahon and an army of 84,000, suffered humiliating defeat and capture. Meanwhile, in Paris, a coup overthrew Napoleon's Second French Empire, and later he and Eugenie escaped to London. Napoleon, a broken man, died soon after.

Bulloz

Bulloz

With the Prussian blockade complete, Paris's only means of communication with the rest of France was by balloon or carrier pigeons. The birds carried microfilm, used to practical effect for the first time. Gambetta made several sorties by balloon in the hope of organizing resistance and a provincial army to come to the relief of Paris. Meanwhile, Parisians launched great public subscriptions to pay for more arms. Victor Hugo, now returned from exile, donated the entire proceeds from his first magazine to the national cannon fund. These new weapons, though, could not assist the French forces outside the city. An aurora borealis which lighted the night

Soon after Sedan the siege of Paris began in earnest. Despite preparations food supplies quickly ran desperately short. Butchers' shops were filled with strange meats, for those that could afford it (above); restaurants offered the most 'exotic' of dishes – elephant trunk vinaigrette, donkey, and angora giblets (above right); and the poor were reduced to raiding the drains in the hope of catching a rat or two (right).

sky in late October turned out to be a harbinger of bad luck – news arrived the next day that Metz had fallen. Still the Parisians demanded *'une resistance à outrance'* (war to the end), in the hope that Gambetta's efforts to raise an army would be fruitful. Initially their perseverence seemed rewarded; news arrived by carrier pigeon that the Army of the Loire had relieved the town of Orleans, defeating the Prussians at the Battle of Couloniers. Paris was ecstatic and talk grew of breaking out of the city to link up with the Army of the Loire. Indeed, the only alternative to breaking out, since Parisians were not prepared to surrender, was starvation.

Provisions grew scarcer by the day. In November the daily mutton and beef ration was reduced to 35 gms (1¼oz) for an adult, and half that for children. 40,000 horses had already been earmarked for slaughter. Cats were displayed in butchers' shops with coloured ribbons and paper frills and described as 'gutter rabbits'. Seasoned and boiled, they were said to be quite tasty. Visitors to the sick were commended to take a dead cat as a welcome alternative to flowers! Outside the famous Hotel de Ville there was even a rat market.

Driving through the Prussian lines, then, seemed

Pioneered by Frenchmen some years earlier, ballooning (right) proved the only means, other than carrier pigeon, for Parisians to communicate with the outside world during the siege. Here, Gambetta makes a night-time sortie to organize a resistance movement and the formation of a provincial army to come to the relief of Paris.

Bildarchiv Preussischer Kulturbesitz

48,000 children, but even this was not enough. Some newspapers hit upon novel sales gimmicks, claiming they could be worn as an undershirt which 'could be worn for a consecutive month without ceasing to be comfortable.'

As the odds stacked higher against Paris, the Prussians played a new card: artillery bombardment. During the first week of 1871, 25,000 shells fell on the city yet casualties were fairly light. But the real ace in the Prussian pack was simply to wait. To add to the miseries of cold and malnutrition came their inevitable concomitant: disease. The siege had forced the people to take drinking water from the polluted River Seine. An epidemic of smallpox and typhoid spread rapidly in the poorer districts to add to the many victims of pneumonia. Mortality was greatest among infants and the elderly.

Breaking point had been reached. The population again clamoured for military action against the Prussians. The military knew such a venture had no hope, but the generals callously felt that national honour would be well served by a last great attack. Indeed, this was what Paris wanted. As the Governor of the city, Trochu, put it, 'Paris must die on her feet.' Coldly and dispassionately, preparations were made for the futile, bloody slaughter of Buzenval Park, launched on January 19. That morning Paris awoke to a new decree ordaining the rationing of bread, but announcing the fresh attack:

'Those of us who can offer their lives on the battlefield will march against the enemy. Those who remain will submit to the bitterest sacrifices.

In a divided atmosphere charged with bitterness and emotion, Paris surrendered and the government collapsed. To make matters worse the Prussians were permitted by the newly elected Assembly to hold a victory march along the Champs Elysées (right).

the only course of action. Gunfire on the night of November 27 announced the attack, but any hope of catching the Prussians off-guard was dashed. French forces reeled under the weight of a massive dawn counter-attack. The battle raged for six days with casualties high amongst the French National Guard. In Paris people waited in the grip of breathless anticipation: great crowds gathered along the Avenue du Trone, but when at last the news came, it was shocking – 12,000 were lost. Ironically news reached Paris just as the orchestra at the opera struck up the triumphal march of Wagner's *Tannhauser*. Three days later the depression was complete: dismayed faces bent over newspapers in Paris which announced the defeat of the Army of the Loire and the recapture of Orleans.

And still Paris refused to surrender. Food shortages forced people to supplement their diets: 'The consumption of dogs, cats and rats is considerable,' wrote one newspaper. Some restaurants offered their clientele more exotic fare. Zebra, Buffalo, Yak, Camel and Elephants found their way on to menus thanks to the entrepreneurial spirit of the director of the Jardin d'Acclimatation. Though food was scarce, there was plenty of wine. Many took to drink hoping to conquer hunger and banish care. The end of December ushered in a new ally to the Prussian cause: the cold. The last week of 1870 was the coldest in living memory with temperatures falling to −12°C. The trees which lined the splendid Bois de Boulogne and Bois de Vincennes were felled when supplies of coal expired. Firewood was rationed to 75 kg a week – not enough to heat a room for a single day during such a bitter winter. Firewood depots were raided by Parisians, while in the Elysée district, telegraph poles were felled. As an act of charity, the Rothschilds supplied the poor with clothes for

Prussian soldiers were entertained in the homes of the Paris bourgeoisie (right) and the government was accused of capitulating to the enemy. This further exacerbated the already divided opinion between the new Assembly and those Parisians who wanted the republic to take a stronger line.

Nationalgalerie, Staatliche Museen Preussischer Kulturbesitz, Berlin (West)

Ingolstadt, Bayerisches Armee Museum. Joachim Blauel, Artothek

Let us suffer, let us die if necessary. Vive la Republique!'

The attack was doomed from the outset as heavy rains turned roads and fields into swamps. Confusion reigned among the French troops which resulted in the accidental shooting of Trochu's escort by his own men. The gloom into which Paris was cast by the appalling debacle was deepened by the news that the last remaining provincial army of General Chanzy had been defeated at Le Mans.

These defeats, and the belief that after four months of siege Parisians would not oppose them, convinced the Government and Army that capitulation was inevitable. Rumours of surrender led hoarding shopkeepers to bring out the last of their hidden provisions, but only the rich could afford them. Cases were reported of people dropping dead in lines outside foodshops. Mortality among children was appalling. One observer wrote, 'At every step you meet an undertaker carrying a little deal coffin.' There were no longer any horses left to transport the dead to their burials, all had been eaten.

Defeat and surrender

The Government decided to seek an armistice. Their representative, Jules Favre, met Bismarck at Versailles. After negotiating an armistice, Favre, with the pride of his defeated capital in mind, told Bismarck that any attempt to disarm the National Guard would be resisted. The German Chancellor uttered this prophetic warning: 'You are making a blunder. There will be heavy reckoning, leaving rifles in the hands of fanatics.' The two sides agreed the bombardment and counter-bombardment cease at midnight on January 26. Bismarck agreed that Paris be allowed the last defiant shot.

The despised Thiers (left), the head of the new Assembly based at the old monarchist seat of Versailles, frustrated the hope held by many Parisians that a new radical republic would emerge from their defeat and the fall of the Second Empire.

defuse the time-bomb in Paris – a volatile situation had been exacerbated by the arrival of 40,000 evacuees in the wake of the Prussian advance. Many prosperous Parisians (including Offenbach) had left before the siege, making Paris more a city of the poor than it had ever been. The final straw came when Thiers announced that all rent arrears built up during the siege be paid in full, and that the National Guard, who had heroically defended the city, would no longer be paid. Many guards relied up on their 1.50 francs a day for basic subsistence. When the government demanded that 200 guns, which had been paid for by public subscription and hidden from the Prussians, be handed over, the National Guard refused. As Bismarck had foretold, Thiers had committed the cardinal blunder of depriving the guards of their pay without having first disarmed them. When two generals of the National Assembly were seized by rioters at Montmartre and hanged, matters quickly got out of hand. The new government felt that revolutionary elements were in control of Paris, threatening to deny their authority while the Prussians looked on.

The Paris Commune

Thiers withdrew, leaving a vacuum filled by the Commune of Paris, which took its name from the Jacobin dominated assembly of 1793. While the governments of the day and many writers subsequently regarded the Commune as inspired by organized left-wing groups, it was rather a populist uprising – a manifestation of outraged patriots, and of general exasperation. The name served as a common

After the fall of Paris, the Prussians offered the French Government a 21 day armistice on condition that a new National Assembly be formally elected on 8 February. Feeling inside Paris was passionately divided. In the election a violent campaign was organized against the 'men of the capitulation', the Government of National Defence. Workers and Extremists were elected along with Republicans. Out of 43 deputies returned, all but 6 were in favour of continuing the war. The result indicated the highly charged emotional state in the capital. Yet the elections in the provinces were overwhelmingly in favour of peace. Not for the first time in French history, the will of the capital and that of the provinces stood out in sharp relief.

The new Assembly on balance was predominantly a monarchist, conservative and provincial affair. It was headed by the 73 year old Thiers, a man whom Parisians hated. As Minister for the Interior in 1848, he had been held responsible for the massacre of Rue Transnovian, when Paris workers had been gunned down by government troops. His appointment rubbed salt into the open wounds of Paris. A series of acts by the new Assembly soon caused the city's latent tendency to insurrection to flare up in exasperation. To begin with, the new government chose to meet at Versailles, the old Bourbon (royalist) centre of government. Paris felt that the hope of a radical Republican administration had been frustrated. To make matters worse, Thiers permitted the Prussians a victory march along the Champs Elysées. This was in return for a reduced war indemnity and France keeping the vital fortress of Belfort. Ever since the suppression of the workers' revolt of 1848 in Paris, many workers had harboured a deep class hatred of the bourgeoisie in general, and of their politician in particular. Adolphe Thiers failed to

rallying point for many disparate groups. If it had one central motive force, it was the manifestation of the living tradition of radical Republicanism. There was thus civil war, and Paris was shortly to undergo its second siege within 6 months – this time by the new French government.

The second battle for Paris began on Palm Sunday, when a government army captured and executed five Communards. The Commune responded by launching a disorganized assault on Versailles which ended in the loss of 1000 prisoners. At this stage the government side had fewer guns and men than the Commune, but Paris failed to press home the advantage. The population, weakened by the first siege were intoxicated by the suddenness with which freedom had come. They could be neither effectively mobilized nor governed. Soldiers turned up for duty much as they pleased while citizens obeyed instructions only when it suited them. Parisians were forever debating, petitioning and celebrating. Lenin later described the Commune as 'a festival of the oppressed'. Theatres and opera went on much as usual, and life went on with far less disruption than during the Prussian siege. Communal legislation was generally moderate. No attempt was made the seize the Bank of France, and private property was not confiscated. The 'Law of hostages' provided for the arrest of those thought to be pro-Assembly, but fighting during the first few weeks was sporadic with relatively few casualties.

The Communards clearly failed to press home their initial advantage. The strength of the Versailles forces grew steadily, while Parisians indulged in the

Edimages

jubilant destruction of the symbols of the old regime. Such acts as the destruction of the Vendôme column, bearing a statue of Lousi XIV, were no substitute for the effective defence of a city surrounded by enemy troops. On 8 May, the bombardment of Paris began afresh. The forts to the south of the city fell one by one. On 21 May, a large section of the city wall was found unguarded, and by nightfall the Versailles army had men inside Paris.

Delescluze, the veteran Jacobin radical of 1848, proclaimed a war of the people, not commanded by officers and discipline, but by the people – rifle in

As Thiers did nothing to defuse the tension between the Assembly and its opponents, the latter set up their own counter-assembly – the Paris Commune (bottom). This was the signal for civil war. To quell the rebels, the Assembly's troops attacked those of the Commune's in the streets of Paris itself (left) – the second siege of Paris was on. As the Versailles troops gained the upper hand, forcing the Communards ever further back behind their barricades, and closed in for the kill, terrible reprisals began. Communards were slaughtered or shot in their thousands by execution squads (below left) until there was no resistance left.

Bildarchiv Preussischer Kulturbesitz

Archiv für Kunst und Geschichte

hand, cobblestone underfoot, and behind the barricades. Only when all was lost did the Commune resolve to fight seriously. Faith in street fighting was unreal. It needed much better organization than a siege operation. Once inside Paris, the Versailles troops, hidden behind buildings and 110,000 strong could only be countered by a planned, watertight defence. Barricades were easily by-passed in the labyrinthine streets.

Bloody week had begun. What was to follow, after the gaiety and lightheartedness of the liberation, was like some appalling fatal accident at the end of a school trip to the seaside. The Versailles troops shot all hostages and generally fought with greater barbarity than the Communards. To the horrors of hand-to-hand fighting was added fire, incendiary shells from the Versailles troops, and the burning of buildings by the Communards to clear lines of fire. The beautiful Tuileries Palace was fired by the rebels as a final act of defiance.

The final few days degenerated into uncoordinated acts of heroism or barbarity. Delescluze, in the dress of a deputy of 1848, top hat, frock coat, girt with his tricolour sash, all being lost, bade his comrades goodbye, and walked quietly down an enfiladed street. In a final act of desperation, he climbed the barricade at the end, stood there a second, then fell forward, shot dead. The novelist, Emile Zola, spoke in horror of 'heaps of bodies piled under bridges – a mass of human flesh dumped at random with heads and limbs jumbled in gross dismemberment.' The last battle took place in the cemetary of Pere-Lachaise, and there on the next day, against a wall that was later to become another shrine of bloody memory in which Paris is too rich, 147 men were shot. Valin, leader of the Commune, was executed after a farcical court marshal. By any standards, the ferocity of retribution is hard to comprehend, let alone condone. As *The Times* of 29 May put it:

The laws of war are mild compared to the inhuman laws of revenge under which the Versailles troops have been bayonetting and ripping up prisoners, women and children. So far as we can recollect, there has been nothing like it in history.

About 20,000 perished in the second siege – more than during the Reign of Terror. Casualties on the government side were light – about 1000. Doubtful of the enduring loyalty of their troops, their leaders moved cautiously, keeping casualties low and morale high. Soldiers were manoeuvred into positions where obedience was the easiest and least dangerous course of action.

Thiers had won a sordid victory. He had tamed Paris. Never again did it decide the fate of the rest of France. The respectable world rejoiced. The fine ladies of Versailles, who had seen Paris burning from the terraces of the palace screamed for more blood. The execution squads were busy. Blood was on the grass like dew. The illusions conjured by the events of Paris's history – 1789-1792 and 1848 – had drawn the people into the most merciless and bloodiest of its defeats. Napoleon III's empire had ended with Paris besieged and France defeated at the hands of the Prussians. But to France's eternal shame, it was an assembly of French monarchists, under a conservative republican head, that first provoked and then put to fire and sword the people of Paris in the bloodbath of May 1871.

Thiers (shown above as the butcher of the Commune) had won a sordid victory in taming Paris. Never again did Paris alone decide the fate of France.

Put to fire and the sword by fellow Frenchmen as well as by Prussia, Paris (represented in the cartoon below) ended 1871 on her knees, defeated and broken by the dogs of war.

THE GREAT COMPOSERS

Johann Strauss II

1825–1899

Vienna in the mid-nineteenth century had long been known as the musical capital of Europe, and the Strauss family dynasty ruled the music halls. Johann Strauss II, the son of a famous father, took up the family business against his father's wishes; soon, his distinctive talents rivalled and quickly surpassed those of his father. Strauss's forte was the waltz, but his gift of melody and his brilliance as an orchestrator were of such high standards that his works sound equally at home in concert halls. The melodic richness and rhythmic variety of his work is perhaps best captured in The Blue Danube, analysed in the Listener's Guide. *All over Europe, high society danced to the music of Strauss, but for a moment, the dancing stopped as the royal tragedy at Mayerling was revealed, as examined in* In The Background. *A prolific writer, Strauss composed nearly 500 works, including operettas and independent concert waltzes. His music is often exuberant, light and sparkling, but always enduring.*

A son in the most famous musical family in the musical capital of Europe, Vienna, Johann Strauss II found little encouragement from his father upon deciding on a musical career, but Strauss soon won over both the sophisticated Viennese audiences and, begrudgingly, his father with his outstanding gifts of melody and orchestration. After his father's death, Johann worked tirelessly, merging his father's orchestra with his own, delegating conducting duties to his brothers, and driving himself to near exhaustion to meet the vast demand for his music. Strauss became known as the 'waltz king' of Vienna, but he also turned his talents to the operetta style of Offenbach, concert waltzes, an opera and an unfinished ballet. His chaotic, hectic life ended in 1899 after a bout of double pneumonia.

'The Waltz King'

Almost all the Strauss family played a part in making Vienna the home of the waltz, but it was Johann Strauss II who was destined to be remembered as the 'Waltz King'.

The child who was destined to eclipse his famous father, Johann Strauss senior, as 'waltz king' was born in Vienna on 25 October 1825. Named after his father and nicknamed 'Schani', he was the eldest of the five surviving children of his parent's marriage. His mother, Anna Strauss, was a woman of strong character and exceptional capabilities, which were later put to the test when her wayward husband departed from the family home to live with his mistress Emilie Trampusch.

Family life

Although there must have been tensions between their parents, there is no record that the young Strausses had unhappy childhoods. Their father was not ideally suited to family life – he was happiest as the dashing public figure of music-maker and conductor. Also, he spent much time away from Vienna and the family, establishing his own reputation and that of his orchestra, abroad.

The family moved twice during Johann's childhood, eventually settling in a large communal house in Vienna, the Hirschenhaus, where they occupied two sets of rooms. To escape from the noise of children, Johann Strauss senior had his own rooms, where he worked and which were often filled with musicians rehearsing his latest compositions.

Summers were spent with the children's maternal grandmother in the suburb of Salmannsdorf. During one of these holidays when he was six Johann composed his first waltz tune, which his mother wrote down and called *Erster Gedanken* (First thoughts).

The three Strauss sons – Johann, Josef and Eduard – all displayed musical talent early in their lives but their father would not hear of them becoming professional musicians. He probably wanted his sons to follow more professional and conventional careers than his own. Although he allowed them to learn the piano he actively discouraged them from any other musical pursuits. Their mother, on the other hand, was greatly encouraging and supportive of their ambitions.

Johann Strauss the younger, ever since he could remember, had wanted to play music just like his father. With his mother's backing Johann began to take lessons in secret from his father's first violinist Franz Amon.

After he turned 11 Johann was sent to the Schottengymnasium, one of Vienna's best secondary schools, which he attended for four years. His father had plans that Johann would enter a banking career, so after the Schottengymnasium he studied at the commercial department of the Polytechnikum.

When his father left the family home and moved in with his mistress, it was clear to Johann that he would probably have to work to support his mother and brothers and sisters. Abandoning the proposed career in banking, he wrote to tell his father that he felt it his duty to support his mother, and that this meant following in his footsteps to become a dance musician.

He resumed his violin studies in earnest and in the open, with the ballet master of the opera, Johann

Anton Kohlmann. He studied theory with a composer of church music, Joseph Drechsler, who naturally enough tried to influence him to become a composer of less secular music.

In the late summer of 1844 Johann felt confident enough to begin his musical career in public and applied to the Vienna magistrate for a licence 'to perform dance music, opera selections and concert pieces, depending on the demands'. He received his licence early in September 1844, formed an orchestra of 24 musicians and then set about finding a venue for his first performance.

Début at Dommayer's

Most of the proprietors of Viennese dance and music establishments had been warned by Strauss senior that they would incur his wrath if they allowed his son to perform in what he liked to think of as his sole preserve. However, with the help of his mother, Johann's début took place at the fashionable and prestigious venue, Dommayer's Casino, in the smart suburb of Hietzing.

Before the performance began most of those present had taken sides – either for father or for the son – but by the end of the evening the audience was completely won over and the Casino reverberated with calls for repeats. Overnight the son became the

Frau Anna Strauss (left) gave her son Johann Strauss II the backing and encouragement he needed to become a professional musician. His estranged father (above, left, shown with his musical contemporary Josef Lanner) did not want his sons – Josef, Johann and Eduard (below, right) to follow him in musical careers. Despite this, all three became closely involved in music-making which was part and parcel of sophisticated society life in 19th-century Vienna (above, centre).

Museen der Stadt Wien

only serious rival to his father and for several years their already strained relationship was to be made more difficult by Johann's success. Sometime later, after a reconciliation of sorts Strauss senior, still unhappy that his son was a competitor, asked him to join his orchestra. Young Johann decided against this, mainly in the interests of his mother with whose help and encouragement he had succeeded in his ambitions, and with whose support he had been able to follow his own path.

Despite his initial success, Johann did not find it easy to support himself and the family in Vienna, so he took his orchestra on tour to the outposts of the Habsburg empire, thereby laying the foundations of his future widespread popularity. The revolution of 1848 added a political colouring to the conflict within the family. Although neither father nor son adhered to any serious political persuasion, it was perhaps natural that the elder man should accept the established order, while the younger sympathized with the rebels and students, many of whom were his own staunch supporters and friends. Schani's part in the revolution did not go far beyond the composition of a *Revolutions-marsch,* although he was arrested by the Police for performing *La Marseillaise* in public! The revolution was quickly put down and the young Emperor Franz Joseph ascended the

Johann Strauss II made his musical début on 15 October 1844 at the fashionable and favourite haunt of many Viennese, Dommayer's Casino (right), in the smart suburb of Hietzing. Overnight he became the only serious rival to his father.

throne. Vienna began to settle down to a comparatively peaceful life-style.

Early in 1849 Strauss senior set off on yet another successful and tiring tour abroad. He returned to Vienna in July 1849 and was soon giving concerts with his usual untiring verve to admiring Viennese audiences. In September he conducted the première of the *Jellachich March* at a concert lasting four hours, which left him exhausted and suffering with a fever. Despite feeling unwell he continued working but a few days later was overcome by the illness. Scarlet fever was diagnosed – he had been infected by the youngest daughter of his mistress Emilie. The child had returned from school ill and had sought comfort from her father, thereby inadvertently infecting him.

Complications set in and on 25 September 1849 Strauss senior died. His mistress disappeared with children, animals and all the goods she could carry away with her, leaving Strauss's corpse naked and untended in a bare room. Anna Strauss and her sons were summoned to the scene by anxious neighbours. Johann was devastated by the scene of his father's death and although through his music he brought joy to himself and countless others, it was said that he was forever after haunted by the morbidity of death.

After the initial shock of the early death of Strauss senior, the Viennese gradually accepted that the son was truly a worthy successor, although not before Johann appealed to public opinion through the columns of the *Wiener Zeitung*.

A meteoric rise

In 1849 Johann merged his father's orchestra personnel with his own and thus began a meteoric rise to international fame. The demand for Johann Strauss and the combined orchestras in the ballrooms of Vienna accelerated, and he was soon obliged to

Johann took Viennese society by storm with his marriage on 26 August 1862 to Henriette Chaluptzky, or 'Jetty' Treffz as she was better known. Jetty (right), several years his senior, was a former singer, who for the preceding 19 years had been the mistress of a wealthy banker, Moritz Todesco. Whatever misgivings there might have been about the bride, she nevertheless proved to be a good wife who brought welcome calm and order into Johann's chaotic life-style.

After his father's death in 1849 Johann took over the conductorship of his father's orchestra and merged it with his own. He was soon in such great demand that he had to employ sufficient musicians to play several venues at once throughout the city. He is shown (far right) conducting one of his orchestras at a Viennese ball, and using his violin bow as a baton.

Although he held no strong political views, it was perhaps natural that during the revolutionary period of 1848 Johann should align his sympathies with the rebels and students. His own part in the revolution, however, did not go beyond the composition of the Revolutions-Marsch, the title page of which is shown above.

employ sufficient musicians to play at several venues throughout the city, while he dashed from one to the other with his violin at the ready to lead a few items at each, thereby justifying the announcements: *'Heut spielt der Strauss!'* – Strauss plays here today! The constant round of composing and rehearsing by day, and playing to an adoring public for half the night eventually took its toll on his health, and in the summer of 1853 he was finally obliged to take a rest cure in the fresh mountain air of Bad Gastein. To ensure the orchestra's continuance with a Strauss at the helm, Johann and his mother persuaded Johann's brother Josef to deputize as interim conductor. Unwillingly, but out of loyalty to the family, Josef left his successful career as an architect and designer. Extremely talented he was no mere second-rate substitute – in fact, he proved so successful in his new role that he never returned to his drawing boards. He died young, aged 43, but in his 17-year musical career produced close on 300 original compositions, none of them in any way inferior to those of his brother.

The following summer saw Johann again recuperating in Bad Gastein, and there he was approached by the directors of a Russian railway company who proposed that he should direct the concerts at Pavlovsk, about 30 kilometres from St Petersburg. The concerts were to take place at the rail terminus, set in a magnificent park, and the plan was to attract more visitors, thus making the railway line from St Petersburg a profitable concern. It was not until the

summer of 1856 however, that Johann travelled to Russia to take up this engagement, leaving Josef in charge of 'the Vienna branch of the family business'. The season marking the first of 12 subsequent visits to Russia, was a great success. Not only were his concerts there successful in terms of popular appeal but they were also highly profitable. It was there in 1869, that Johann and Josef shared not only the conducting, but also combined their talents to produce the famous *Pizzicato Polka*. By that time, their youngest brother, Eduard, was also established as conductor and composer in partnership with his brothers.

Romance and marriage

It comes as no suprise that the handsome and successful Johann Strauss enjoyed a number of love affairs, and it was in Russia that he first took one of them seriously enough to contemplate marriage; but the aristocratic parents of the lady in question, Olga Smirnitzky, would not hear of it. Unabashed, Johann transferred his affections elsewhere. Two years later on 26 August 1862, Johann's friend and publisher Carl Haslinger received a note from him:

Dear friend Haslinger, shameless fraudulent soul of a book printer! Will you come to my place at 7 o'clock tomorrow morning, to support me at my marriage one hour later? Answer immediately, you inky-fingered music dabbler! Jean.

The one-time Schani had become known by the

more fashionable name of 'Jean' and his bride to be was Henriette Chalupetzky, formerly a renowned singer known professionally as 'Jetty' Treffz. Jetty was the mother of several children and for the preceding 19 years had lived as the mistress of the wealthy banker Moritz Todesco. The Strauss family and all Vienna were astounded by the news, but whatever the misgivings Jetty proved to be a good wife, secretary, manager and artistic adviser. She brought order into Johann's hitherto hectic life-style, encouraging him to take more time over composition and to delegate more work with the orchestra to his brothers. Thanks in part to Jetty's steadying influence during the 1860s Strauss created many of his greatest waltzes, such as *Morgenblätter* (Morning Papers), *Künstlerleben* (Artist's Life) and *Geschichten aus dem Wienerwald* (Tales from the Vienna Woods). A year after his marriage to Jetty, Johann was granted a title he had sought many times and which his father had held before him: that of K.K. Hofballmusikdirektor (Director of Music for the Imperial and Royal Court Balls).

In 1864 relations between Strauss and his publisher, Carl Haslinger, deteriorated over financial matters. For a time Strauss may have considered entering publishing himself. Haslinger tried to persuade other publishers to boycott all three Strauss brothers, but finally C. A. Spina broke the boycott and became Strauss's new publisher.

Every year at Carnival time the Strausses were in great demand and the season of 1867 was no exception. The renowned Vienna Men's Choral Society, the Wiener *Männergesangverein,* wanted a new work to present at their annual *Narrenabend* (Fools' Evening). Reminded of an earlier promise to write something for this choir, Strauss set about reworking a rough draft he had found among his papers. By tradition the Fools' Evening was a riotous affair in fancy dress, but in 1867 the mood of Vienna was comparatively subdued. The populace was still reeling from the military defeat of Austria by Prussia at Königgrätz. The Imperial Court Ball that year was replaced by a formal concert and the *Männer-*

During the 1860s Strauss wrote many memorable waltzes including The Blue Danube *and the* Wiener-Chronik *waltz (title page shown above).*

During the autumn of 1867 Johann and Jetty visited London to take part in a season of Promenade Concerts which were performed at the Royal Italian Opera, Covent Garden (left). The season was a huge success with uproar and exultation at the end of every performance of waltzes.

Every year at Carnival time in Vienna Strauss was in great demand. Traditionally the festivities were riotous fancy dress affairs, like the Fools' Evening of the Vienna Men's Choral Society (below). In 1867, however, suiting the subdued mood of a defeated country, the festivities took on a more formal aspect. Strauss wrote The Blue Danube *waltz for the concert which, that year, replaced their fancy dress evening.*

gesangverein followed suit.

Strauss's composition – *The Blue Danube* – which was his first choral waltz, started the second half of a mixed programme on 15 February at the Dianasaal. It was well received but wasn't accorded the half-dozen or more repetitions that so many Strauss works received. It was, however, destined to become his most popular waltz and with it he established his reputation in Paris later in 1867.

Strauss abroad

Strauss chose to make his début in Paris during the World Exhibition of 1867 and although the Strauss Orchestra was committed to engagements at home under the direction of Josef and Eduard, Johann reached an agreement with the German conductor, Bilse, who undertook to provide an orchestra in Paris and to share the conducting with Strauss. In Paris,

Johann and Jetty quickly established contacts that were to ensure the most prestigious engagements. Of all the social events held in connection with the Exhibition, the most lavish was the Gala Ball given at the Austrian Embassy by the Ambassador's wife, Princess Pauline Metternich. Jetty wrote home to Vienna:

Jean is the lion here, there has been no comparable success here for years, it is a fever, a tremendous triumph. Proposals are coming in, America is already in view – fabulous, fabulous!

One proposal that Johann immediately accepted came from London. The 25-year-old Prince of Wales had been impressed by the Waltz King's music and personality, and had apparently recommended him to Mr John Russell, who was to present a season of Promenade Concerts in London during the autumn of 1867. The 'classical' repertoire would be conducted by Giovanni Bottesini, the virtuoso double-bass player, and Strauss would conduct several of his own compositions at each of the 63 concerts scheduled to be given from 15 August to 26 October at the Royal Italian Opera, Covent Garden.

Jetty Strauss was no stranger to London – she had appeared there as soloist with Johann Strauss senior during his visit in 1849. Although she had long ago given up her stage career, she sang at ten of the Covent Garden concerts, sometimes accompanied by Johann at the piano, her repertoire including *Home, Sweet Home,* some Scottish songs, and arias by Mozart and Mendelssohn. We also learn from Johann's diary, in which he kept a detailed record of the London concerts, that the *Annen Polka* achieved no fewer than 82 performances during the season, its closest rival being the *Tritsch-Tratsch Polka,* played 38 times.

Johann and Jetty must have been well satisfied with their visit to London, for Johann closed his diary with the words: 'Splendid jubilation such as I have *never* known in my life!!! The most beautiful concert of my career! Vivat the English from the bottom of my heart!'

No doubt influenced by his encounter with Offenbach's stage works and encouraged by his wife and friend Max Steiner, the director of the Theater an der Wien, Strauss began to compose for the theatre after 1870. Of the many operettas he wrote, at least 13, including Der Zigeunerbaron *(left), had their first performances at the Theater an der Wien (centre). Many were successful but lacked good librettos, and as a result it is mainly the music, rather than texts, which has survived.*

Museen der Stadt Wien

Museen der Stadt Wien

On returning to Vienna, Johann retained more than a pleasant recollection of his London concerts, he regarded them as a pattern on which to re-style his Soirées, and began a new series of concerts at the Floral Hall of the Vienna Gardens Association. So much did England impress Strauss that when in 1869 he bought a house at Hietzing, near Dommayer's, he furnished and decorated it as if it was an English home.

A new direction

In 1870, aged 45, Johann was at the peak of success and popularity when he suffered the loss of his mother, who had always been the influential guiding star of the 'family business'. Less than six months later, his brother Josef, the shy, retiring, reluctant

genius of the family, died after collapsing while conducting in Warsaw. The principal conductorship and day-to-day management of the Strauss Orchestra passed to the youngest brother, Eduard, who was to uphold the tradition until he disbanded the orchestra in 1901. Leaving Eduard to direct the family orchestra freed Strauss to accept invitations to conduct outside Vienna, and he took up offers in London, Budapest and Paris. More importantly, though, it freed him to pursue a new musical direction – with operetta – but he had to be pushed into it.

Strauss had already come across, and admired, the operettas of Offenbach. Indeed, Offenbach had even advised him to try his hand in this sphere. But Strauss was not keen to start. He knew himself well enough to know that he had no innate ability when it came to working with words and drama, and he appreciated that it demanded a particular talent to combine words, music and theatre successfully. With hindsight his reluctance seems justified as nearly all his ensuing operettas were let down by his poor choice of librettos. Nevertheless, he was eventually persuaded by Jetty and Maximilian Steiner, the director of the Theater an der Wien, to compose for the stage.

In 1872 Jetty and Johann attended the World's Peace Jubilee and International Music Festival in Boston, USA (left). Johann conducted a vast orchestra and chorus before an audience which he estimated at 100,000.

Strauss's third and greatest operetta, Die Fledermaus (title page of one of the waltzes from it, far left) was produced in 1874.

Museen der Stadt Wien

In order to obain a divorce to marry his third wife Adele Strauss (left), Johann had to become a Protestant, give up his Austrian citizenship and take on that of the Duchy of Saxe-Coburg-Gotha in 1886. Nonetheless Strauss's music continued to reflect the gaiety and glamour of his beloved city of Vienna (above).

Strauss writes for the stage

In May 1870, Johann entered into a contract with the Theater an der Wien, the first fruit of which was the operetta, *Indigo und die vierzig Räuber,* (Indigo and the Forty Thieves). The première was fixed for 10 February, 1871; Maximilian Steiner's co-director, the popular soprano Marie Geistinger, sang the leading role and Strauss conducted. The house was sold out and the management had even improvised some additional seating. As in the case of some of the subsequent operettas, the text did not make good theatre, and only the music survived the success of the first few years.

Before completing his second operetta *Der Carneval in Rom* (Carnival in Rome) he and Jetty set sail for America in June 1872. Their destination was Boston, where the impresario Patrick S. Gilmore had organized a World's Peace Jubilee and International Music Festival. Johann's role was to conduct a vast orchestra and chorus before an audience which he estimated at 100,000! The outcome was hardly artistic, but the rewards, both financial and in terms of prestige were considerable.

By the end of January 1873 'Carnival in Rome' was in rehearsal at the Theater an der Wein. It was followed in 1874 by *Die Fledermaus.* Although its first season was not entirely smooth, *Die Fledermaus* was a masterpiece. There were frequent inter-ruptions in the run to allow for previously scheduled appearances at the Theater an der Wien of the renowned singer Adelina Patti, and eventually, after the 49th performance of the operetta, it was taken off due to illness among the cast.

According to some sources Jetty and Strauss entered a difficult time in their marriage. Jetty who was in her 60s was no longer the vivacious hostess of former times, nor did she go out much. There appeared also to be disagreements over finances. In April 1878, however, Jetty Strauss suffered a stroke and died. Johann was stunned and at first unable to cope alone with any aspect of life that was not directly connected with music, yet within two months he was married again: this time to 28 year-old Angelika ('Lilli') Dittrich. It was a disastrous union and it ended in separation after four years. His third marriage was to a young widow, Adele Strauss (the daughter of the family financial adviser). In order to marry Adele who was Jewish (he was a Catholic), he had to renounce his Austrian citizenship. Consequently he took citizenship of the Duchy of Saxe-Coburg-Gotha in 1866, became a Protestant, and therefore obtained a divorce.

Happy last years

His last years with Adele and her daughter Alice brought him the peace and contentment that his highly strung temperament needed. He continued to compose not only operettas, the greatest of which after *Die Fledermaus* was *Der Zigeunerbaron* (The Gypsy Baron) in 1885, but also some of his finest independent concert waltzes, including the coloratura *Frühlingsstimmen* (Voices of Spring) and the magnificent *Kaiser-Walzer* (Emperor Waltz). There was also an opera, *Ritter Pasman,* that was produced at the Vienna Court Opera but withdrawn after only nine performances.

Throughout his last years, honours of all kinds were showered on the 'waltz king', who all the while remained modest and unaffected. He liked to pass the time when not composing in a game of cards or billiards with some of his close friends, among whom were the pianist Alfred Grünfeld, the surgeon Theodor Billroth, the sculptor Victor Tilgner, the great operetta comic Alexander Girardi, and of course, Johannes Brahms.

In May 1899, Johann caught a chill which very soon developed into the double pneumonia that was to end his life. He took to his bed but continued to write music, working on his only full-length ballet score, *Aschenbrödel* (Cinderella). He never finished but after his death the score was completed by Josef Bayer, the director of ballet at the Court Opera.

On the afternoon of 3 June 1899 Adele persuaded her husband to try and sleep a little; he replied: 'I will certainly do that . . .' At a quarter past four he died, peacefully sleeping.

After a funeral procession through Vienna he was buried on 6 June in the Central Cemetery in a grave near to those of the city's other great musical luminaries – Brahms, Schubert and Beethoven.

Archiv für Kunst und Geschichte

The silhouette caricature (left) drawn after Strauss's death shows him conducting a celestial waltz. Not only are the musical cherubs enchanted by his music, but so are some of the other musical inhabitants of heaven. Those who cannot help joining in the waltz are Haydn, Schumann, Mozart, Bruckner, Handel, Bach, Liszt, Wagner, von Bülow, Brahms, Chopin, Schubert and Beethoven.

Waltzes

In the glittering waltzes that came cascading from Johann Strauss's pen lies sparkling and enduring music – as attractive for the listener as it is entertaining for the dancer.

In 1843, the year before Johann Strauss began conducting his own orchestra, an Austrian writer observed that the Viennese . . .

seem to any serious observer to be revelling in an everlasting state of intoxication. Eat, drink and be merry are the three cardinal virtues and pleasures of the Viennese. It is always Sunday, always Carnival time for them. There is music everywhere.'

Vienna had long been the musical capital of Europe; Mozart, Beethoven and Schubert were among the numerous composers who made it their home. But the Viennese had often responded with indifference to the greatest works of such masters. Serious, profound music had limited appeal for them; what they wanted was a good tune — preferably that one could dance to. The Strauss family provided such tunes in abundance, and Johann Strauss the younger became the personification of the city's musical spirit.

It started with the waltz. Early in the century, when the craze for this new dance was in full swing, the first Johann Strauss and his friend — and rival — Joseph Lanner began composing music for it. Each had his own orchestra — Lanner's in the Prater amusement park and Strauss's in the Sperl dance hall — and a following of enthusiastic and insatiable dancers to satisfy. The waltzes they composed were a considerable improvement on earlier models, being made up not merely of one tune but of several, joined in a varied sequence and often preceded by an introduction and rounded off with a coda. Besides speeding up the tempo from its original, rather sedate pace, both composers introduced variations on the simple one-two-three beat, such as cross-rhythms and syncopation, which made it less repetitious.

While sharing such innovations in waltz-writing, the two composers each had a distinctive style: Lanner's hallmark was strong melody, while Strauss emphasized the rhythmic momentum. Whereas the music of Lanner, according to popular opinion, said, 'Pray dance, I beg you,' that of Strauss said 'Dance, I command you.' He became known as the 'Father of the waltz'.

And so, when the younger Strauss first picked up his baton in 1844, leading a band of 24 musicians, the waltz was not only the most popular dance in Vienna (and the rest of Europe) but also an established musical form — one that he was to develop to a high degree of sophistication. His early waltzes were very like those of his father's, being marked by their lively rhythm and pace, but in later years he showed more of the lyricism of Lanner and successfully fused the two styles to create waltzes of sheer perfection.

Waltzes to order

Like both his father and Lanner, Strauss often had to compose in a hurry. The giddy whirl of Viennese social life, with one ball after another, created a constant demand for new dance music. Looking back on the hectic days of his early career, Strauss wrote that it was sufficient . . .

to have an idea. Strangely one always had one. Our self-confidence was such that we would often announce a new waltz for the evening, though not one note had been written in the morning.

In such a case the orchestra appeared at the composer's home. As soon as one part of the waltz was composed, the musicians would arrange and copy it. A few hours later the whole piece was ready. It was then rehearsed, and would be performed in the evening for an enthusiastic audience.

Fortunately, Strauss had a facility for melodic invention almost on a par with Schubert's. Musical ideas flowed effortlessly from his brain. He would scribble them down on anything that was to hand — a menu, his shirt cuff, or even a bed sheet. Unlike his father's tunes, which tended to be short, his were broad, expansive melodies — singable as well as danceable.

This melodic richness is one explanation for the fact that Strauss's dance music was, and still is, popular in the concert hall. Each of his waltzes contains at least five distinct melodies — many of them eight or

By the 1890s the once-shocking waltz was ultra-respectable and made more popular than ever, particularly in high society (left) by the music of Johann Strauss II. Strauss's waltzes encapsulated perfectly the carefree spirit of the Austrian capital in the reign of the Emperor Franz Josef. More than just dance music, they later appealed to concert audiences because of their melodic richness, rhythmic vitality and sparkling orchestration.

more. These do not contrast sharply with each other, as do symphonic themes, for example, but grow out of each other, giving a sense of progression that must have been appreciated, if only subliminally, by dancers. In fact, dancers at balls in Vienna and elsewhere sometimes stopped to listen to the music.

Another reason for the popularity of Strauss waltzes in the concert repertoire is their rhythmic variety. Many of them open with a slow introduction – often containing bits of melodies to come – which creates a feeling of anticipation and serves as an effective contrast for the exuberant burst of waltz tempo music that follows. Acceleration is also used effectively to build up excitement and to free the music from the rigid mould of the basic waltz rhythm.

Strauss's genius for orchestration is yet another reason for his enduring popularity. In his day it was admired by some of his greatest contemporaries, including Brahms and Wagner. (Incidentally, Wagner's *bête noir,* the critic Eduard Hanslick, also criticized Strauss for, among other things, his 'highly sophisticated

The opening bars of 'The Blue Danube' (left) are perhaps the most famous of all waltz themes. Shown left is a facsimile of the composer's manuscript. One of Strauss's admiring colleagues, Brahms, once used the theme when autographing a fan belonging to Strauss's wife, adding the words, 'Unfortunately not by – Johannes Brahms'.

The cover of the first edition of 'The Blue Danube' (below), arranged for piano, shows the celebrated river flowing through a dramatic landscape, complete with castle. But the music is really about Vienna and has become a sort of unofficial Viennese anthem. Ironically, it was originally detested by the Viennese.

harmonies'.) Clarity of texture and brilliant use of instrumental colours are two of its hallmarks. Brass and woodwinds often figure prominently, and percussion, such as bells, cymbals and drum rolls is often used to good effect.

But Strauss wrote most of his music originally for his own instrument, the violin, and this is apparent in the arrangements for full orchestra. The violin's range of colours and techniques, such as pizzicato and double stopping, are brilliantly exploited. The waltzes, especially, have a lyrical 'singing' quality associated with the violin.

There is also a trace of melancholy in the sound of a violin, and this quality in Strauss's music gives an added dimension to the picture of Viennese life that it portrays. For the air of frivolity that pervaded the city masked an awareness of the uncertainties and tragedies of life. Strauss himself was prey to various fears and had an extreme dread of illness and death, and in his music he managed to express not only the Viennese love of beauty and zest for life but also, if only fleetingly, the consciousness that all the festivities must sometime come to an end. Today, when the splendours of the Hapsburg empire are only a dimly-remembered dream, Strauss's exhilarating music has acquired additional poignancy.

Programme notes

Among the pieces analysed in the following pages – waltzes and other works by Johann Strauss – are very widely illustrative examples of some of his best-loved and best-known music. Here are the graceful melodies, the full-blooded exuberance and the wistful nostalgia that will always evoke the spirit of Vienna in its heyday.

The Blue Danube

Ironically, when the Viennese first heard this waltz they did not like it. There are two good, non-musical reasons for this. At the time, 1867, the mood in the city was depressed, mainly because of the crushing

military defeat Austria had suffered at the hands of the Prussian army the previous year. The waltz as we know it today might have lightened that mood, but on this occasion it was performed with a male voice choir singing verses which had been specially composed for the occasion by an amateur poet (by profession a police official) which went, in part:

Viennese, be gay,
Oho, why, why?
A glimmer of light –
We see only night.

In German the words sound equally fatuous. The Viennese were not amused, much less cheered; the choir, in fact, had almost refused to sing it.

Once the 'silly' verses had been shed, however, *The Blue Danube* (whose title Strauss derived from a line of poetry by Karl Isidor Beck) became a runaway success. At a ball given at the Austrian embassy in Paris a few months later, Strauss conducted the orchestra in his new waltz – this time to great acclaim. The Parisians adored *Le beau Danube Bleu*: any subsequent ball was considered incomplete without it. Other countries also took it to their hearts. Over a million

'In the Harem' (above) sums up the rather sentimental view of the Orient which comes out in Strauss's operetta A Thousand and One Nights.

copies were sold, making a fortune for the publisher, Spina, who had had thousands of copies made a few months after its failure in Vienna and had distributed them all over the world. Strauss, in fact, received only a hundred or so guilders for it. Soon, though, with its increasing popularity, the Viennese adopted the once-despised waltz as virtually their unofficial anthem. The opening notes of its main theme are recognized around the world:

The theme first appears in the slow introduction, played on muted brass and woodwinds with a shimmering string accompaniment, suggesting the leisurely flow of the river itself. After a brief interruption by another sprightly tune, it reappears in a stately tempo, gradually accelerating into the full, swirling waltz. It is followed by a profusion of other melodies – by turns cheerful, nostalgic and lusty. The coda brings back the main theme, first in its stately form, then in short variations, eventually subsiding into the reflective mood of the opening. A typically Straussian flourish brings the waltz to a close.

Pizzicato Polka

After the waltz, the polka was probably the most popular dance of the mid-nineteenth century. It originated in Bohemia and was introduced to Vienna in 1839. The derivation of its name is uncertain, but it may come from the Czech word for a Polish girl, *polska*. With its bouncy two-four rhythm, the polka never entirely lost sight of its folk origins: where the waltz is elegant, the polka is energetic and high spirited.

Strauss's *Pizzicato Polka,* which he wrote in collaboration with his brother Josef, is a witty little concert piece, as frothy as Viennese whipped cream. Played by the strings entirely *pizzicato,* and punctuated occasionally by tinkling bells, it suggests a polka danced on tiptoe by playful elves.

Roses from the South

This waltz contains some of Strauss's most memorable tunes and interesting contrasts of mood. The introduction begins with a gliding, bittersweet melody that later returns twice in the main section. This begins with a rollicking theme in Strauss's most engaging manner:

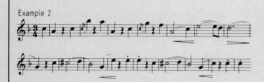

The melody is borrowed from one of Strauss's unsuccessful operettas, *Das Spitzentuch der Königen (The Queen's Handkerchief),* which concerns an improbable story about the Spanish writer Cervantes and the Queen of Portugal. In the operetta this music is used for the

In Tales from the Vienna Woods, *Strauss conjures up a musical scene of a 'heuriger' – one of the wine houses found in the woods outside Vienna (above).*

'Truffle Couplet', in which the King praises his favourite food.

The waltz ends with a rousing 'drinking song' type of tune, belted out on the brass with great gusto.

The Hunt

Even more strenuous than the polka is the galop which was popular in Vienna in the 1820s. Its brisk two-four beat later achieved more lasting identity as the basis for the can-can.

Though *The Hunt* is not a true galop, it is a lively toe-tapping piece that, along with several other of Strauss's compositions (such as *The Tritsch-Tratsch Polka*), has a strongly equestrian flavour.

With typically clever use of percussion – including salvos of gunfire – Strauss recreates the excitement of a chase on horseback through the woods and fields outside Vienna.

A Thousand and One Nights

Like *Roses from the South,* this waltz draws upon material that Strauss first used in an operetta. Originally called *Indigo and the Forty Robbers,* the operetta suffered, like many of his others, from a bad libretto – in this case written by a team. In the Vienna coffee houses the current joke was that the 'forty robbers' were the forty plagiarists who had cobbled the story together.

The music, however, was lovely and the operetta a great success. Its first performance, at the Theater an der Wien, marked the beginning of the 'golden age' of Viennese operetta. Eventually a new story was written for *Indigo* and the piece was re-titled *A Thousand and One Nights.* The operetta is now sometimes given under this newer name, rather than 'Indigo'.

The waltz of the same name opens with a rather reflective introduction, containing fragments of the tunes that reappear, fully formed, in the main section. Despite the occasional burst of high spirits, this waltz has, predominantly, a somewhat wistful character.

Echoing the themes in the music, the title page of 'Tales from the Vienna Woods' (right) shows various country pursuits, including also a folk zither player. Strauss used this instrument in the introduction to the waltz.

Despite the title Egyptian March, Strauss's music is a robust European march containing only a dash of the type of flavour expected (below).

Tales from the Vienna Woods

Second only to *The Blue Danube* in popularity, 'Tales from the Vienna Woods' is in many people's opinion an even finer piece of music. Its most striking feature is the long introduction, a miniature tone poem depicting the contrasting moods and pastimes of the countryside surrounding Vienna. Strauss once said that his talent was born of the city around him, 'where the sounds that fill the air and ring in my ears, I took in with my heart and wrote down with my hand.' Strauss's great love of the leafy Vienna woods is evident here in the subtle way he interweaves the various melodic fragments and contrasting colours, including distant hunting horns, birdsong and snatches of lively folk dance — some reminiscent of neighbouring Hungary. Most evocative of all is a hunting ländler tune played on a zither, which conjures up the atmosphere of a *heuriger,* — one of the country inns outside the city where city-folk gathered to sit in the open and taste the fresh young wines that these inns offered.

Understanding music: the waltz

The waltz as the world knows it, with the impulsive first beat and that seductive lilt on the second two (varying according to country) had its true natural source in the world of the folk dance. The basic folk dance from which it evolved was the Austrian ländler, a dance in 3/4 time. The new 'waltz' development became fashionable among sophisticated urban people in the late 18th century, and its infectious um-pom-pom rhythm, now greatly emphasized, caught the imagination of many classical composers, such as Beethoven, Brahms, Schubert and Chopin.

In the famous Sperl dance hall in Vienna, opened in 1807, the waltz became all the rage. In the Apollo, opened soon after, 6000 dancers at a time could be found disporting themselves to 3/4 time. It was natural that such a demand should produce composers who specialized in their needs. Schubert used to frequent these halls to hear the music of Michael Pamer (1782-1827) and Joseph Lanner, and influenced by his visits, wrote a vast number of waltzes for the piano. The waltz became the chief glory of Viennese operettas, led by Johann Strauss II and his masterpiece, *Die Fledermaus*. Who does not know and love the rich waltzes that Franz Lehar (1870–1948) put into such works as his immortal *The Merry Widow* (1905), *The Count of Luxembourg* (1909) or *Gypsy Love* (1910). They were such an expected feature that one of the remarkable things about the later *Land of Smiles* (1929) was that its main song 'You are my heart's delight' was *not* a waltz.

Strauss took the waltz to Paris in the 1850s but there was already a master of the art there – Jacques Offenbach. Although few think of him as a waltz king, many of the finest songs in his operettas are beautifully poised and poignant waltzes. Paris had another waltz exponent in Emil Waldteufel (1837-1915) who, as pianist to the Empress Eugénie, kept the society balls supplied with vivacious, Frenchified waltzes, where the accent unlike the Viennese waltz, was on the first beat. *Les Patineurs* ('The Skaters'); *Estudiana* and *The Grenadiers* rival the finest Viennese confections with their wit, charm and *joie de vivre*. In Copenhagen, the famous Tivoli Gardens were reigned over by Hans Lumbye (1810—74) who became a 'Northern Strauss'; but though Victorian England, after some resistance, succumbed to the charms of the waltz, there was no British composer of waltzes of equal standing.

Though the waltz conquered the ball room, classical composers were not slow to exploit the waltz for mere listening pleasure. One of the first such essays was Weber's 'Invitation to the Dance' written in 1819. After the invitation is beseechingly made by the solo cello, the music bursts into a riot of amazingly forward-looking waltz themes that Lanner and the Strausses would have been proud to lay claim to. Brahms continued on the path of Schubert by writing a series of beguiling piano waltzes and, in vocal form, some joyful part songs which he called the *Liebeslieder* waltzes. Chopin took matters further in his piano waltzes by making them emotional adventures ranging through every mood. Some of the most sumptuous waltzes ever written became the heart and soul of Richard Strauss's opera *Der Rosenkavalier* (1911) and Ravel, having toyed with the waltz in a meditative way in his piano *Valses Nobles et Sentimentales,* attempted a symphonic work that would glorify the Viennese waltz as never before. Originally intended to be called *Wien,* it became simply, *La Valse.*

When the waltz was first danced some elements of society were scandalized to see that it involved close physical contact between partners. Following pronouncements on the dance's harmful moral effects, the waltz became the subject of many an amusing cartoon (left).

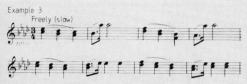

Example 3
Freely (slow)

In the main section the ländler theme is transformed into a waltz, appearing just after the sunny opening melody. It reappears, again played by the zither, in the coda.

Egyptian March

Although less well-known than many of Strauss's other compositions, this piece is a delightful example of his humour and musical ingenuity. It is about as Egyptian as Mozart's opera *The Abduction from the Seraglio* is Turkish – making no more than a gesture towards ethnic authenticity. The opening and closing few bars do suggest the 'mysterious East', and a chorus contributes a bit of pseudo-Arabic vocalizing, but the toe-tapping rhythm and extrovert colour show clearly that the title is not to be taken seriously.

Wiener Blut

Literally 'Vienna Blood', the title of this waltz is better translated as 'Spirit of Vienna', carrying as it does the notion that to have Viennese blood coursing through one's veins would make one strong and spirited. After Strauss's death, this waltz was incorporated into an operetta of the same name. As is often the case in Strauss's waltzes, some of the most interesting writing comes in the introduction: this one contains a soulful passage for strings that is later developed into the robust main waltz theme.

Picking flowers by the River (left) has the same fresh, joyous character as Strauss's waltz Voices of Spring. *The waltz was not*

Perpetuum Mobile

Another piece with an interesting title, *Perpetuum Mobile* literally means 'perpetual motion' and is a musical interpretation of the scientific idea that it might be possible to invent a machine that would continue to work indefinitely. Strauss's version of the idea is a sprightly galop, orchestrated with dazzling colour, which whirls around and repeats its theme with seemingly endless energy. But this creates a problem: sooner or later the players must stop, and thus make a nonsense of the title. On one occasion, Willi Boskowsky, then conducting the Vienna Philharmonic Orchestra, found an ingenious solution. Towards the end of the piece the voice of the conductor was heard calling out in German *'un so geht es immer weiter'*–'and so it goes on and on'.

Voices of Spring

Like *The Blue Danube,* this waltz was not immediately popular in Vienna. Strauss wrote it originally as a coloratura aria for a soprano called Bianca Bianchi, who sang it at the Theater an der Wien to a lukewarm reception. Critics found it 'mediocre' and 'not very melodious'. Later, however, it enjoyed great popularity in Russia and Italy, and finally in Vienna as well. A famous pianist, Alfred Grunfeld, adapted it for his concerts; and an even more famous pianist, Franz Liszt, was one of its great admirers.

In contrast to the other waltzes in this collection, *Voices of Spring* has no introduction, but plunges right into its giddily spinning main theme. Although it does not have the melodic profusion of *The Blue Danube,* for example, it is one of the most light-hearted and joyous of all Strauss waltzes. A particularly charming touch is the use of the harp in the coda.

an immediate success in Vienna, but a piano adaptation by Alfred Grunfeld helped in its renewed popularity.

FURTHER LISTENING

Die Fledermaus

This was Johann Strauss II's third operatic work, and proved to be not only his masterpiece, but the most enduring operetta to come out of either Austria or Germany during operetta's golden age. The plot is impossibly complex and full of elaborate deceptions, but it is all good fun and a real joy for the audience from beginning to end. The good-hearted secrecy and hoaxing which fills the plot is all made credible by the wonderfully rich portraiture Strauss achieves through his music.

Der Zigeunerbaron

The Gypsy Baron, as it is known in English, was a considerable success for Strauss and has remained in constant demand ever since.

Many of its arias, as well as its overture, are often played or sung in concert halls and are perennially popular, especially in Germany. There are also many authentic touches of Hungarian music and rhythms throughout this work – more than in *Die Fledermaus,* as is appropriate for a story with a Hungarian setting.

Other dances and marches

All of the Strausses – Johann II, his father, and Josef – composed great quantities of marches and dances for all sorts of occasions. These include not only waltzes and polkas but also quadrilles, galops and mazurkas. Much of this music repays close attention, as it is by no means all froth and toe-tapping rhythms.

'The little Vetsera'

The music of Johann Strauss is indelibly linked with the image of a resplendent Vienna, but in 1889 Viennese society was rocked by the scandal of the century – the tragedy at Mayerling.

Archiv für Kunst und Geschichte

Prince Rudolf (above), the heir to the Austrian throne who died at Mayerling, shooting first his young mistress, Mary Vetsera, and then himself.

On the night of 29 January 1889, Crown Prince Rudolf, the 30-year-old heir to the Hapsburg Empire of Austria-Hungary, shot first his teenage mistress, Mary Vetsera, and then himself in a bedroom in his small hunting lodge at Mayerling, deep in the wooded country surrounding Vienna. Early in the following morning the bodies were discovered and the horrific news was rushed to the imperial palace, the Hofburg, in Vienna. No one could face telling the emperor, so the Empress Elisabeth, whose Greek lesson had to be interrupted, was told before him of the heir apparent's death. At first she wept bitterly, but then, drawing herself up with remarkable composure, she went to tell her husband, the Emperor Franz Joseph.

The scandal of the century
At the imperial family's request, the police, the prime minister (Count Taaffe) and the court doctor immediately went into action, their first priority being to cover up the most scandalous aspects of the Crown Prince's sudden death, namely the fact that it had been caused by suicide, and the presence of Mary Vetsera's corpse.

Mary Vetsera's furtive funeral was a macabre, inhuman affair. When she had been dead for a day and a half, her body, which had neither been washed nor laid out, was propped up in a carriage between two of her uncles and taken along icy roads at night to the nearby village of Heiligenkreuz. There, the local abbot had been persuaded to agree to her burial in the graveyard under his jurisdiction, despite Catholic scruples about burying suicides in consecrated ground: Mary's official death certificate stated that she had taken her own life, for it could hardly read 'shot dead by the Crown Prince Rudolf'. On the next morning a howling gale delayed the actual digging of the grave – Mary's uncles had to help the gravediggers – but the authorities were satisfied that the whole operation had gone ahead without attracting undue notice. This satisfaction was premature, however, for although there were no journalists in the vicinity, the locals could not help noticing all the curious comings and goings, and Mayerling was to become one of the hottest news stories of the century.

Love and death
In Vienna the first official announcement in the morning newspapers stated that the crown prince had died of a heart attack, but nobody believed this. Apart from his age, it was generally thought (incorrectly) that Rudolf had been in reasonable shape physically, and so far more interesting rumours immediately began to circulate about how, why and with whom he had died.

A day later, the emperor authorized a second official announcement, informing the public of at least part of the truth. This second statement said that the Crown Prince had taken his own life with the aid of a revolver and it mentioned a 'malformation of the skull' to suggest that he had done so under acute mental strain – this was the only way of guaranteeing Rudolf a full Catholic funeral, for a suicide could only get such treatment if he were proven to have been of unsound mind.

But, coming after the heart attack story, this announcement was just too straightforward to be believable, and the very fact that such a different version of things had been officially announced first encouraged further speculation. Also, too many of

The lovely, vivacious but rather empty-headed daughter of the wealthy Baltazzi family, Mary Vetsera (right), was barely 18 years old when she went to Mayerling to die with the prince she adored too much.

Archiv für Kunst und Geschichte

the people involved with the cover-up at Mayerling and Mary Vetsera's funeral talked, and within a week of the tragedy aspects of Mary's involvement had begun to percolate out into the sea of rumour and gossip that now absorbed Vienna. Despite the fact that there had only been two short official announcements, and that was to be all, and the fact that Mary Vetsera was not mentioned in either of these statements, what had happened at Mayerling soon became common knowledge. But interpretations of the tragedy differed according to people's sympathies, or their proximity to direct sources of information.

Even today, a precise reconstruction of the events leading up to Mayerling is a matter of guesswork because the findings of the court commission of inquiry and the official autopsies on the bodies have never been found, and because many of the central participants in the aftermath lied in their accounts of what happened in order to exonerate themselves from any blame. But the simplest and most obvious 'explanation' for the events at Mayerling went as follows.

Rudolf and Mary were deeply in love but he was unhappily married to Crown Princess Stephanie and, as the Hapsburg heir apparent and a Catholic, was unable to obtain a divorce to marry Mary (who may have been pregnant). Therefore, like the Tristan and Isolde of Wagner's new opera, which was all the rage

Rudolf and Mary died together on the night of the 29 January 1889. Less than 24 hours later, Rudolf's body was taken hastily from Mayerling under cover of night (left) and carried to the Hofburg in Vienna. Later the following day, 31 January, Mary's body was propped up in a coach between two of her uncles and taken, again under cover of darkness, to be buried in a local churchyard. But these attempts to cover up the real nature of the tragedy were doomed to failure.

News of the Crown Prince's death rocked Viennese society and on the morning of the 31 January, the streets of the city buzzed with men and women exchanging gossip and passing comment (right). No-one really believed the official explanation – that Rudolf had died from a heart attack – and rumours about the involvement of Mary Vetsera soon began to circulate.

The tragedy at Mayerling was hot news not only in Austria, but all over Europe, and over two weeks later The Illustrated London News *was still supplying readers with stories on the background to the tragedy (right). On this front page is part of Rudolf's family: his wife Stephanie, his only child Elisabeth and his Uncle Karl and cousin Francis.*

at the time, the lovers decided to take their own lives rather than end their relationship, or endure its continuation in secret.

This romantic interpretation is probably the one Mary would have hoped for. Not yet eighteen and head over heels in love with her prince, it is quite likely that she offered to die with Rudolf because the alternatives were too unbearable. Since she couldn't live without him, she would die with him.

But Rudolf was well-known as a bit of a rake and it seems unlikely that 'the little Vetsera' would have been a major passion. In fact, less than 48 hours before his death, he had been sleeping with another woman, Mitzi Caspar, a former dancer and singer of light songs at the opera who had become a prostitute. Rudolf was one of Mitzi's 'regulars' and, according to her, he had once asked her to join him in a death pact too. So, for Rudolf, a less romantic explanation had to be sought.

The Wittelsbach madness

Ironically, the expedient 'unsound mind' that ensured a full church funeral for Rudolf does appear to have had some basis in truth. Several latent conflicts in Rudolf's life – involving politics, marital difficulties, family tensions, excessive drinking and general ill health – probably combined to demoralize him so thoroughly that he lost all sense of proportion and went ahead with the deed he had frequently talked of. There is some evidence, too, from the diaries and reminiscences of people who knew him and letters he wrote, that Rudolf often feared he was on the brink of madness, and that he

Rudolf's mother, the Empress Elisabeth (far left) loved her husband, the Emperor Franz Joseph (near left) dearly, even though their marriage had been arranged. But she found the Viennese court unbearably claustrophobic and her liberal political views made her a liability to her husband. Elisabeth was allowed to 'escape' from court life and spent much of her life travelling yet she continued to influence her son. Her uncertain position and her volatile nature undoubtedly contributed to Rudolf's emotional instability.

often spoke of his death as the only 'honourable' way out of the personal problems he felt overwhelmed by. Moreover, a fear of hereditary insanity stalked the imperial family, particularly Rudolf's mother the Empress Elisabeth who was herself a very unstable person.

Elisabeth was one of the Wittelsbachs, the Bavarian royal family, who were so intermarried with the Hapsburgs that the empress and emperor were first cousins, and their children only had half the usual number of grandparents. 'Mad' King Ludwig of Bavaria was one of Elisabeth's cousins and she lived in dread that the family weakness would manifest itself again. (Elisabeth did in fact blame the tragedy at Mayerling on the Wittelsbach affliction.)

The empress had been brought up in a relatively happy-go-lucky household that did little to prepare her for the rigours of her married life as the first lady in the most ancient and protocol-ridden court in Europe. She was an extremely beautiful woman – no portrait was said to do justice to her allegedly 'supernatural beauty' – and Franz Joseph worshipped her. But after the birth of her third surviving child (Rudolf was the second), the only way in which Elisabeth could cope both with her imperial responsibilities and her in-laws, notably her overbearing mother-in-law, the Archduchess Sophie, was by frequent 'travelling'.

In contrast to his wife, and ever mindful of his survival of the revolutions in the year of his accession, Franz Joseph was as intensely conservative and unimaginative as he was shy and conscientious. Acutely aware of his responsibilities as the head of the 600-year-old Hapsburg dynasty, he worked incredibly hard, far harder than any of his civil servants, but had little time for new ideas. It seemed to him that the old ways were tried and true, and as a result the Hapsburg court was the stuffiest in Europe. Despite this conservatism, however, Franz Joseph was a kindly and compassionate man, an old-fashioned 'gentleman' to the core.

For Rudolf, Franz Joseph's conservatism was

stifling. He had had a far more liberal education than his father and had a natural curiosity in new ideas. And from his wayward mother, he had inherited a love for travelling and a sympathy for the Hungarian nationalist cause which could only bring him into conflict with his father. Indeed, he often found his political differences with his father and his father's political advisers so frustrating that he would act as a 'mole' on official policies to journalists, leaking information about government tendencies he disapproved of and sometimes writing articles anonymously. The political straightjacket of his role as heir to the throne could only exacerbate his natural instability.

A disastrous marriage

Neither did Rudolf's marriage, which had been arranged with purely dynastic and religious considerations in mind, help. Despite the shrewd misgivings of the Empress Elisabeth, Franz Joseph had pursued the only match he could condone for his son, marriage with one of the few remaining catholic-born princesses of late 19th century Europe – Princess Stephanie of Belgium. By all accounts, Stephanie was rather stupid, bossy and plain, hardly compatible with the highly educated and fastidious Rudolf who, though not considered to be handsome in a conventional sense, was nonetheless rated as a charming and 'pale and interesting' personality.

Rudolf and Stephanie were married in 1881 when she was just sixteen and he was twenty-three, and he allegedly became a noticeably gloomier person from the time of the marriage onwards. In the years before Mayerling, it was noticed that he seemed to become less and less well. Early in 1886 he became mysteriously ill and a retrospective analysis of his symptoms and the treatment suggests strongly that he was afflicted with syphilis. A year later he became very ill with bronchitis and could only contain violent fits of coughing by taking 'injurious' doses of morphine. In the following spring inflammation of the eyes assailed him, and kept him from shooting parties, and in the summer of 1888, after a riding accident, he began to suffer from severe headaches.

The treatment for syphilis was painful and, in those days, seldom completely effective. But Rudolf's complaint was called cystitis and peritonitis, and poor Stephanie was not told otherwise. She only found out the true nature of Rudolf's affliction, when she succumbed to the disease herself. Naturally enough, discovery of the true nature of the illness, and probably the realization that it meant no more children (their only child was born in 1883), did little to ease tension within the marriage.

Such 'dynastic' marriages, like Rudolf and Stephanie's, where the object was to create a bond between families, rather than individuals, were quite common. And under such arrangements husband and wife often agreed to go their separate ways within the marriage – but not so Stephanie. Unlike other royal wives – Britain's Princess Alexandra, for example, who managed the playboy Prince of Wales's indiscretions without rancour – Stephanie was reluctant to turn a blind eye to Rudolf's infidelities. She did not accept his amorous deviations as a fact of royal life and was apparently furious at the blatant way in which the affair with Mary Vetsera was conducted. Stephanie was one of the few people to whom Rudolf sent a farewell note, and it allegedly began:

Dear Stephanie,
You are rid of my presence and tiresomeness; be happy in your own way . . .

A fatal 'crush'

If Crown Princess Stephanie's attitude upset Rudolf, his affair with the young Mary Vetsera was hardly likely to restore his equilibrium. She was barely educated, completely spoilt and brought up to think only of clothes, horse racing and pleasure. When she was sixteen (the age when she probably first met Rudolf), her mother began to take her out to society gatherings and she immediately attracted attention because of her ravishing 'oriental' beauty and her vitality; the Prince of Wales (later King Edward VII), who met her at a race meeting in 1888, found her pretty and charming.

Mary's mother, Baroness Helene Baltazzi-Vetsera, was the daughter of a Levantine banker who had amassed a great fortune in Constantinople and then settled in Vienna. She was an extremely ambitious woman socially and was considered, in the jargon of the day, to be rather 'fast'. (In fact she was once suspected of having amorous designs on Rudolf herself.) By marrying a minor diplomat she had climbed up a rung on the social ladder, but she was determined that Mary should secure their position with a really brilliant match. And, in the late 1880s, it looked as if her hopes would be realized, for Mary was surrounded by aristocratic suitors, including the Duke of Braganza. Rudolf, too, seemed interested and, provided this didn't go too far, could only enhance Mary's prospects. But the baroness reckoned without Mary's consuming passion for Rudolf, and her skill in keeping the details of the affair from her family.

Long before she met him properly, Mary had developed an enormous 'crush' on Rudolf. She seldom kept her eyes off him at social gatherings and her obsession had become a Vetsera family joke. And since Rudolf liked to conduct his amorous affairs on the principle of the newer the better, it was

Insanity seemed to run in the interbred Hapsburg family, and it may have been fear of going mad that drove Rudolf to take his own life. His mother Elisabeth's cousin, for instance, was 'Mad' King Ludwig of Bavaria (right) who drowned in mysterious circumstances – possibly as a result of suicide.

Bildarchiv Preussischer Kulturbesitz

The closing years of the Hapsburg Empire were beset by tragedy. In 1898, it was poor Elisabeth, 'the vagabond empress', who was the victim. Boarding a steamer in Geneva, she was attacked by a wild-eyed young man, the Italian anarchist Luigi Luccheni (far left). After the attack, with immense willpower, she walked onto the boat, saying nothing of the stab wound inflicted by her assailant. But the knife had pierced her heart – within an hour she was dead. Despite her errant nature, she was much loved by her husband and by the people of Austria, and her funeral in Vienna (near left) was a grand state occasion.

inevitable that he eventually responded to the extremely flattering attentions of this beautiful young woman.

Several months after the Mayerling affair, Helene Baltazzi-Vetsera had a brochure privately published in which she gave her account of the circumstances that had led to Mary and Rudolf's deaths. The tragedy had ruined her socially and in this work she was attempting to defend herself from accusations that, by turning a blind eye to her daughter's liaison because of her hope of using the imperial connection in some advantageous way, she had somehow been responsible for what happened.

In her defence Baroness Vetsera reproduced her daughter's farewell letters, which clearly showed a determination to do something mysterious and serious, but she protested that she was ignorant of the extent of Mary's involvement with Rudolf and of her fatal intentions. She dated the actual seduction to about two weeks before Mayerling and accounted for Mary's conspicuous obsession with Rudolf during the previous year by maintaining that this was still only the 'crush' stage of the affair. But the worldly baroness must have known more; for example, she could hardly have failed to notice the expensive presents Mary received from her princely paramour. It is more probable that the baroness was quite used to dealing with precarious situations, and that she hoped to retrieve Mary before she became too entangled. Helene Baltazzi-Vetsera would not have approved of a full-blown affair because there was absolutely no hope of a marriage, and she would probably have been genuinely horrified had she known that at some stage late in 1888 Mary became Rudolf's mistress. (Indeed, it is quite possible that Mary bolted for Mayerling because her mother had just discovered the full story and was endeavouring to end the whole relationship.)

The road to disaster

The tragedy at Mayerling began on the evening of 27 January, when the whole of Viennese high society, including the Baltazzi-Vetseras and members of the imperial family, were gathered at a reception given by the German ambassador in honour of the Kaiser's birthday. At this function Rudolf took the opportunity to plan a shooting trip with his friend Count Hoyos. He asked the count to arrange with Prince Philip of Coburg (Rudolf's brother-in-law) to be in Mayerling for breakfast on the 29th. Mayerling was the Crown Prince's private hunting lodge, 2½ hours from Vienna. Lit by oil lamps and decorated with hunting trophies, it had excited little interest from Crown Princess Stephanie, who seldom went there.

When the hunting party assembled on the morning of the 29th, Rudolf excused himself from the day's activities because of a cold. Then Rudolf must have rejoined Mary, who had 'disappeared' from her home the day before.

Mary had vanished while her chaperon, Countess Larisch, was in a shop and she had been left sitting in a carriage outside. According to contemporary gossip, Countess Larisch had herself once been in love with the Crown Prince, and she so resented his marriage to Stephanie that she was only too willing to act as Rudolf's 'go between' with Mary Vetsera, frequently acting as her young charge's alibi or escorting her to places where propriety demanded a married lady as a companion.

But on this particular shopping expedition, when the countess returned to the carriage to find Mary gone, she was sufficiently alarmed – Mary had been behaving strangely and dropping dark hints about her intentions in the previous days – to alert Helene Baltazzi-Vetsera. Convinced that Mary was with Rudolf at Mayerling, they went together to the Police Chief Krauss, who was known to be in charge of

On 28 June, 1914, yet another Hapsburg met an untimely end when the Archduke Franz Ferdinand was shot and killed in Sarajevo by Gavrilo Princip, photographed here as he was led away from the scene of the assassination (right). Ferdinand's death became the final trigger that launched Europe into the Great War, a war that was to complete the destruction of the house of Hapsburg.

'minding' Rudolf. But Krauss explained that the hunting lodge was the Crown Prince's personal property and therefore beyond his jurisdiction. Even so, he quickly informed the prime minister, Count Taafe. Taafe was sceptical about Baroness Vetsera's sudden motherly concern about her daughter's activities and, far from seeing a murderous situation developing, only considered the possibility of something mildy risqué happening.

On the evening of the 29th a family dinner party was scheduled to take place at the imperial palace in Vienna to celebrate the engagement of Rudolf's sister Valerie. Philip of Coburg duly left Mayerling to attend this party, arranging to return early in the following morning to continue the shoot. Meanwhile Rudolf simply sent a message to Stephanie, asking her to excuse his absence due to a heavy cold. In fact he dined that night with Count Hoyos, who later claimed that the prince had had a good appetite and had seemed in good spirits despite his cold. At around nine o'clock the friends said goodnight, and retired to their respective quarters (as an old crony of Rudolf's, Hoyos probably suspected that he had a ladyfriend somewhere on the premises). But early next morning a valet found Rudolf and Mary's bodies slumped in their bedroom, and by midday a distraught Count Hoyos had reached Vienna with the terrible news.

A portentous tragedy
By eight o'clock on the morning of the following day the coffin containing Rudolf's body had reached the Hofburg. Now the emperor knew from the court doctor the full horror of Rudolf's death and, wearing full uniform with sword and gloves, he went to see the body. A full autopsy began that evening, and on the following morning the way in which Rudolf had really died was told in the second official announcement to the public.

The funeral took place on 5 February, on a cold and grey winter afternoon. The coffin was taken from the Hofburg, where the body had been lying in state (with cosmetic wax filling the huge hole in the skull made by the bullet wound), through the narrow streets of the old city of Vienna, to the Church of the Capuchins. When the ceremony was over it was carried down to the crypt and Rudolf was laid to rest among his Hapsburg ancestors. By the imperial family's request, no other crowned heads were present apart from the King and Queen of Belgium, Stephanie's parents. Franz Joseph managed to contain his grief until he followed the coffin to the crypt, where he broke down and wept – the empress had been too distraught even to attend the funeral.

Franz Joseph's courage and dignity throughout this time earned him universal admiration and sympathy. Typically, he coped by retiring even deeper in to his official shell and surrounding himself with even more work, reserving his affection and confidences only for his family, a very small entourage and his great friend, the actress Katharina Schratt. But the death of 'our dear Rudolf whom we shall never forget' hurt him profoundly and then, in 1898, there came another great blow – his beloved wife, the Empress Elisabeth, was stabbed to death by a lone wolf anarchist while on one of her trips abroad.

These unhappy events seemed portentous to many people in Vienna. It was widely believed that when *'der alte Herr'* (the old Gentleman) died, so too would the Hapsburg Empire of Austria-Hungary. Furthermore, the untimely death of Crown Prince Rudolf, with his go-ahead inclinations and modern-mindedness, was of shattering significance for Austria-Hungary. The new heir apparent, Archduke Franz Ferdinand, was not very popular and when he was assassinated at Sarajevo in 1914 the First World War which resulted in the disintegration of the old empire, was precipitated. Mayerling was more than a great human tragedy, it was also of immense political import, for on that bleak January night Austria-Hungary not only lost a crown prince, it also lost its future.

THE GREAT COMPOSERS

Claude Debussy

1862–1918

The French composer Claude Debussy found his genius in experimentation; in his evocative works, he tried to liberate music from conventional forms. Even as a student at the Paris Conservatoire, he worked with musical ideas in new and controversial ways. When he began to compose in earnest after winning the Prix de Rome, he became absorbed in reworking the basic materials of music and re-analysing the roles of the symphony orchestra to express new ideas and images. Debussy's revolution began when, inspired by the influences of Impressionist painters and Symbolist poets, he developed an 'impressionist' style of music. The profound influences of Impressionism and Symbolism are discussed in In The Background. Perhaps his most famous impressionist work is La Mer, and its evocation of the eternal mysteries of the sea is analysed in the Listener's Guide. Debussy's great musical imagination made him one of the most influential figures of his generation and his style continues to influence composers profoundly.

Claude Debussy's early life was unsettled, with no formal education and little sense of home. He entered the Paris Conservatoire in 1872, but Debussy soon abandoned his piano studies and turned to developing his growing fascination with composition. He lived a penniless but cultured, bohemian life and his openness to the influences of the Symbolist poets with whom he shared his time soon found outlet in his music. Debussy was revered in the artistic community as the composer of the moment, a role at odds with his own deeply private character. Under the spell of the Impressionist movement in painting, his most creative works emerged. The bohemian world was left behind as he achieved artistic acclaim. A diagnosis of cancer in 1909 pushed Debussy into activity; his last years saw a revived output of great emotional power. He died in Paris in 1918.

COMPOSER'S LIFE

'Rotten with talent'

Debussy's life was chequered, to say the least, yet he was destined to rise, after inauspicious beginnings, to lead the world of music in a new and exciting direction.

The French composer Claude-Achille Debussy (left) was born in Paris and spent most of his adult life in the Bohemian quarter of Montmartre (below).

Claude-Achille Debussy was born in Paris on 22 August, 1862, the first of five children. The household was a poor one, his father, Manuel, being generally irresponsible in both money and family matters. His mother, Victorine, also regarded herself as a free spirit and spent most of her time trying to forget she ever had any children. Consequently, the young Claude and his brothers and sisters were frequently packed off to Cannes, where, in the home of their aunt and godmother, Clémentine, they were largely brought up. She not only gave them all much-needed love and attention, but was also the first to note Claude's attraction to music and arranged for his first piano lesson.

The unsettled nature of Claude's early life must have reached a climax in 1871, the year of the Paris Commune, when his father was arrested and imprisoned. During this period Manuel Debussy met Charles Sivry whose mother, Madam Antoinette-Flore Mauté, convinced him of his son's musical talent. This cultured and intelligent woman – the mother-in-law of Verlaine – immediately recognized the young boy's talent at the keyboard and declared that he must be trained for a concert career.

Manuel, seeing visions of a life of leisure being supported by his genius son, gave up his plan that Claude should be a sailor and enthusiastically agreed.

Mansell Collection

Debussy's parents expressed little concern for the welfare of their children and, in fact, passed much of the responsibility for their upbringing to Clémentine Debussy – the children's aunt and godmother. Consequently, Debussy and his brothers and sisters had an unsettled childhood moving between Paris and Cannes (left) where she lived. Here, Debussy spent much of his time until he entered the Paris Conservatoire.

During Debussy's student years his piano teacher, Marmontel, arranged summer work for him as house musician to various wealthy patrons. The first appointment was at the opulent Château de Chenonceaux (below) – the home of Madame Marguerite Wilson-Pelouze.

Debussy met Madame Blanche-Adélaïde Vasnier (right), a singer, in 1881. It has been suggested, though not proved, that they had an affair. Undoubtedly, though, Debussy was deeply attached to her and dedicated to her many of his early songs.

So the nine-year-old Claude was groomed by Madam Mauté for entry into the Conservatoire. She lavished care and attention on him to such an extent that he became almost a grandchild to her, and he frequently stayed at her apartments.

Debussy responded well to such encouragement, passing the 1872 summer exams for entrance into the Conservatoire. A measure of Madame Mauté's achievement here is shown by the fact that to this date Debussy had received no formal schooling.

Early training

Debussy thus started his music training as a piano student with Antoine Marmontel, and for the first three years made good progress. At a Conservatoire concert of 1875 he was described as having 'a delightful temperament . . . this budding Mozart is a regular devil.' However, within three years he was to give up all pretensions to a career as a virtuoso, for he was rapidly becoming fascinated by composition. After a second prize for piano in 1877 there were no more pianistic awards.

As Debussy's piano studies waned, his music theory successes multiplied and he began to experiment with sounds and musical ideas in novel and often controversial ways. Although he was an unorthodox student interested in anything which challenged existing musical beliefs, he always made sure he did enough work on the basics to sustain high examination marks. Thus a first prize in 1880 for practical harmony enabled the eighteen-year-old to progress to the composition class.

Meanwhile, in the previous summer, 1879, his world had opened up in a new and exciting way. His old piano teacher, Marmontel, managed to find him a summer post as house musician to the cultured millionairess and Wagner fanatic, Madame Marguerite Wilson-Pelouze. He spent the summer months at her beautiful and opulent home, the Château de Chenonceaux.

The summer of 1880 found him in even more sumptuous surroundings, for Marmontel placed him

with Nadezhda von Meck, the wealthy Russian patroness of Tchaikovsky. For this and the following summers of 1881 and 1882, Debussy became part of the von Meck household, playing to the family, accompanying them, and tutoring some of Madame von Meck's substantial brood of children. He travelled throughout Europe with them, and seems to have been very popular as both accompanist and tutor.

Exposure to the leisurely and sophisticated life-style enjoyed by such wealthy people obviously stimulated Debussy greatly, and lead him to dream of similar surroundings for himself. Not surprisingly, Madame von Meck was the first person to be presented with a composition by the ambitious young man. This she forwarded to Tchaikovsky for his comments. His judgement was crushing: 'It's a very nice thing but really too short; nothing is developed and the form is bungled.' Thus ended Debussy's first attempt at wider artistic recognition.

Montmartre life

Meanwhile, life and study continued back in Paris. His composition studies progressed to the satisfaction of his teachers, and Debussy gradually discovered a sympathetic circle of like-minded young artists with whom to spend his evenings. He frequented many of the new Montmartre cabarets with companions such as the composers Erik Satie and Paul Dukas, and the poet Raymond Bonheur. Together they encountered the new poetry of the great Symbolist writers such as Verlaine, Mallarmé and de Banville as it was being created. It was these poets, and others like them, who were to provide Debussy with inspiration for some of his greatest music in years to come.

It was around this time, particularly, that Debussy became acutely self-conscious of his appearance – he was short, swarthy and solidly-built, with a thick mop of black wavy hair and the most extraordinary forehead, caused by two protuberances formed by benign tumours on the bone. These crowned his

BBC Hulton Picture Library

head at the hairline and attempting to hide them he combed locks of hair down over them in a 'girlish' fringe.

Another important friendship at this time was with the wealthy amateur singer, Madame Blanche-Adélaide Vasnier, a beautiful woman married to a civil servant eleven years her senior. Soon after their first meeting, Debussy was virtually living in the Vasniers' apartments. Many of his songs from this time were dedicated to Blanche, and it is often suggested that they had an affair. Whatever the case, their relationship was temporarily interrupted by Debussy's move to Rome.

In 1884 he entered, and won, the Conservatoire's *Prix de Rome*. Part of the prize was four years of subsidized study and unsupervised composition with accommodation at the Villa Medici in Rome. Although this was what he had wanted for years, shortly after his arrival he was implacable in his hatred of the villa, his fellow prize-winners from previous years, and Rome itself. Only one event stirred any enthusiasm in him: a meeting with the aged virtuoso Franz Liszt. Liszt encouraged Debussy to seek out performances of the music of Renaissance masters such as Palestrina and di Lasso in the little churches of Rome. When he finally made the effort, the young Frenchman was immediately won over. But from every other aspect he found Rome 'positively ugly – a town of marble, fleas and boredom'. At the start of his third year he could take no more. He hurriedly wrote a letter of resignation to the Conservatoire and bolted back to Paris and the Vasniers.

Back in Paris he produced the major work required of him by the rules of the *Prix de Rome,* the cantata *La damoiselle élue* set to a poem by Dante Gabriel Rossetti. This, his first mature work, was condemned by the Conservatoire though it appeared not to worry him as by then he had other things on his mind. He was practically penniless, and had no reason to believe things would improve. Nevertheless, he moved into his own Montmartre garret and began looking for wealthy patrons. He also

Pinelli 'Santa Maria dell'Anima'. Museo di Roma/Mauro Pucciarelli-Rome

started to lead a cultured, bohemian lifestyle in earnest, taking up all the latest literary, artistic and musical fashions, and arguing constantly among his friends about the relative merits of their contemporaries. Somehow he even found the time and money to go to Bayreuth, Bavaria, in 1888 to see Wagner's *Parsifal* and *Die Meistersinger,* yet his feelings towards Wagner's achievements were to remain deeply ambivalent for the rest of his life.

Oriental influence

However, the 1889 Paris World Exhibition was to expose Debussy to an influence he wholeheartedly embraced: Orientalism. At the exhibition, he was transfixed by the strange rituals of the Cochin China Travelling Theatre, and he spent hour after hour in the Javanese section 'listening to the percussive rhythmic complexities of the gamelan (xylophone) with its inexhaustible combinations of ethereal, flashing timbres'. This far-Eastern influence permeated much of his work and thinking for the next twenty years. In this he was not alone, for his contemporaries in art and literature, including such diverse figures as Gauguin, Zola and Manet, were just as enthusiastic in their appreciation.

The early 1890s, ironically, found Debussy irresolute and unproductive. It was 1893 before he produced a work, his *String Quartet op. 10.* But it was well worth the wait – one critic commenting at its première that Debussy was 'rotten with talent'. The Quartet hardly made him a household name, however, and he continued to live in an aimless and hedonistic fashion. During this time, though, he did make a string of notable aquaintances including the young poet and aesthete Pierre Louÿs, Oscar Wilde, and Marcel Proust.

Then, almost suddenly, the tide began to turn. His love of Mallarmé's poetry bore spectacular fruit with his *Prélude à l'après-midi d'un faune,* composed as a musical equivalent of Mallarmé's famous symbolist poem. This one perfect and revolutionary piece was enough to alter the course of music in France. Mallarmé himself marvelled at it: 'your illustration . . . presents no dissonance with my text; rather does it

Debussy won the Prix de Rome in 1884 and was awarded four years of study in Rome. Although it was the realization of a long-held wish, he found little enjoyment in his stay. His one pleasure, though, was listening to the Renaissance music which could be heard in Rome's many small churches (above). After two years he abandoned the 'city of marble, fleas and boredom' and returned to Paris, taking up the bohemian lifestyle of Parisian artistic society. Here he encountered, and was greatly inspired by, the poetry of a group known as the 'Symbolists' (right).

go further into the nostalgia and light (it) with subtlety, malaise and richness.' The work was successful across Europe and, though it brought in no money, it established Debussy's name outside Montmartre. He himself seemed totally unconcerned, continuing to live in penury with his mistress while relying on the generosity of a few friends such as Louÿs and patrons such as the publisher Hartmann. Thus thanks to their generosity he continued work on his new opera, *Pelléas et Mélisande,* and gradually gathered around himself most of the little comforts in life.

Marriage to Lily Texier

This lifestyle was to remain more or less the same up to the première of 'Pelléas' in 1902, but there were some decidedly desperate moments in between. Most of them involved his affairs with women. His relationship with the strong-willed, beautiful and passionate Gabrielle Dupont – his mistress – was a stormy one. More than once she left him, or he left her for a brief fling with someone else. In 1897 her discovery of just such a fling led to an attempted suicide with more than a hint of the melodramatic. By 1899 the pair had literally worn each other out, and when Debussy quietly slipped off with the

Fantin-Latour 'A Corner Table'. Musée d'Orsay, Paris/Réunion des musées nationaux

In 1893 Debussy met the young poet Pierre Louÿs (right) who was to become one of his closest friends during the ensuing decade. Sadly, their friendship did not survive after Debussy (photographed by Louÿs, far right) left his first wife, Lily, to live with Emma Bardac, whom he subsequently married. Like many of Debussy's friends, Louÿs suspected that Debussy's motives were purely financial.

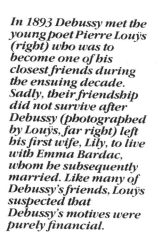

simple and pretty Rosalie (Lily) Texier, it was with Gaby's blessing. The new couple were married in October of the same year.

The première of *Pelléas et Mélisande* marked the real watershed in Debussy's career. This setting of Maurice Maeterlinck's symbolist play produced a completely new type of opera — one which had a poetic as well as a musical intention. Its effect was to make Debussy the composer of the moment, the leader of a new 'school' called 'Debussyism', and something of an institution. All of this he greeted with intense dislike, surliness and distrust, for he remained a deeply private man, committed to his own creative path, with no use for public curiosity.

Still, for better or for worse, his life was irrevocably changed. For one thing, he was no longer completely dependant on the charity of friends or on the income from the musical critiques he had begun to write for different journals in 1900 under the name of Monsieur Croche. 'Pelléas' was the start of his ascent to self-sufficiency. On the domestic front the changes were even more sweeping.

Debussy elopes

At the end of 1903 he met Emma Bardac, a beautiful and distinguished Jewish heiress with children from her first marriage and a seemingly wealthy future on the death of her millionaire uncle. Debussy fell madly in love with her and, in 1904, the two eloped — prompting Lily Debussy into a suicide bid.

Lily survived, as had Gabrielle Dupont in 1897, but Debussy's behaviour killed many of his closest friendships, including that of Pierre Louÿs, as his motives were seen as purely financial, considering Emma's own personal fortune. But two subsequent events bear witness to the inaccuracy of this accusation: one is the birth out of wedlock the following year of Claude-Emma (Chou-Chou). The other is their marriage in 1908: the year after Emma was disinherited by her uncle for taking up with a musician and four years after the start of bitter divorce proceedings by Lily.

'Debussyism'

Thus there was a considerable moral, financial and artistic strain on Debussy as he prepared for the première of a new work *La mer,* in 1905. Happily, the work was an immediate sensation, despite an inept performance at the première by a conductor who became lost in the score. Overnight, Debussy had created, and became the leader of, a new school – that of musical 'Impressionism'. However, Debussy did not follow an exclusive 'impressionist' line in his music – he was interested in the eternal mysteries evoked by nature as well as by its representation. In this he was more in step with his Symbolist contemporaries and it is significant that his greatest unfulfilled wish was to write an opera to the Edgar Allan Poe short story *The Fall of the House of Usher* – Poe was easily one of the greatest influences on the French Symbolists and Decadents.

The two years after this triumph, despite the security afforded by Emma's own resources, were a major trial to Debussy. During this period he saw the virtual disappearance of his old lifestyle, and most of his old friends with it. He was deeply disturbed by such wholesale loss, and wrote virtually no music at this time. His only compensations were Emma and Chou-Chou, to both of whom he was devoted.

The marriage, in 1908, though, seemed to galvanize Debussy into activity and from this time until his death, his creative fertility was astonishing, and he turned his hand to virtually every musical form. He also took up a career as a conductor of his own works, urged on by numerous requests from impresarios as well as by his own desire for financial independence. Unfortunately, he was a very poor conductor, and the constant rehearsals and concerts were an agony for him. Nevertheless, the public did not seem to notice his lack of conducting prowess and the concerts were a popular success.

By 1909 the first symptoms of cancer of the rectum had been discovered and from 1912 onwards Debussy suffered almost daily haemorrhages. Resorting to mixtures of cocaine and morphine to suppress the pain he persevered with the conducting tours, and also started accepting commissions for orchestral works in the hope of earning quick money, dedicated as he was to providing his wife and daughter with a real measure of security.

Debussy's revived creativity led to collaborations with two extraordinary personalities in 1911–12 – the impresario Sergei Diaghilev and the Italian playwright Gabriele d'Annunzio. Considering the impact of Diaghilev's *Ballet Russes* on Paris in 1909 it is not surprising to find Debussy eager to work with him. Yet it took them four years to mount an original ballet together. Their first project, a choreographing of *Prélude à l'après-midi d'un faune,* was a dismal failure which Debussy himself cordially detested.

The composer's collaboration with d'Annunzio hardly fared much better. D'Annunzio had arrived in Paris in 1911 in a blaze of publicity as the greatest living Italian playwright come to Paris, and he had come especially to write a 'mystery play' on the death and martyrdom of St Sebastian. In reality, he had fled from Italy to avoid paying his many creditors for his extravagant lifestyle. On his arrival he immediately recruited the famous actress Ida Rubinstein for the part of the saint, and asked Debussy to supply the musical interludes. Debussy's fine and often deeply moving score notwithstanding, the work was a disaster. The première itself seems to have been almost farcical in its failure. Even *Jeux,* the

ballet produced with Diaghilev in 1913, failed to win general acclaim. This, Debussy's last orchestral masterpiece, was made a nonsense of by Nijinsky's childish and narcissistic choreography. And within two weeks of its première it was more or less buried by the scandal and controversy surrounding the first night of a work by Debussy's friend Stravinsky: *The Rite of Spring.* In the orgy of critical recrimination provoked by Stravinsky, the more refined and delicate audacity of *Jeux's* score was completely overlooked.

During 1913, the year before the outbreak of the Great War, Debussy continued his battle against his illness, completing both a round of conducting engagements and new sets of compositions. Both books of *Preludes* for piano were completed, as well as the second of his two piano suites for his daughter, Chou-Chou. This in itself was significant, for it is clear that his domestic life was deeply fulfilling for him, both with his wife Emma and with his beloved daughter, who was by all accounts a beautiful and vivacious child.

Debussy's setting of one of Mallarmé's poems, **Prélude à l'après-midi d'un faune,** *was given its first performance to tumultuous acclaim in 1894. In 1909 Debussy collaborated with the impresario Sergei Diaghilev to produce a ballet to this music. The famous Russian dancer Nijinsky (above) danced the lead part at the ballet's première, but his choreography, rather than the music, contributed to its dismal failure.*

MUSICA

MADEMOISELLE MAGGIE TAYTE
Dans le rôle de Mélisande, du Pelléas et Mélisande de Claude Debussy et Maurice Maeterlinck, qu'elle vient d'interpréter, à l'Opéra-Comique, avec beaucoup d'art et un grand succès.

The impact of war

The outbreak of war in August 1914 put an immediate stop to Debussy's public engagements, and also temporarily stilled his creative impulse. His reactions to France's involvement were markedly ambivalent:

'I have nothing of the army spirit – I've never even held a rifle. My recollections of 1870 and the anxiety of my wife, whose son and son-in-law are in the army, prevent me from developing any enthusiasm.' In a later letter he wrote: *'if, to ensure victory, they are absolutely in need of another face to be bashed in, I'll offer mine without question ... (however) ... Art and war have never, at any period, been able to find any basis of agreement.'*

Debussy's publisher, Durand, aware of his reduced income brought on by the war, gave him a new edition of Chopin's works to edit in early 1915. This was to bear glorious fruit later that year when Debussy wrote the twelve *Etudes,* his crowning pianistic achievement. As the year wore on, other works in a new, severe style poured from his pen. Struggling as he was by this time against the cancer which had a terminal grip on him, he managed to complete two of a projected set of six chamber pieces, as well as *En blanc et noir,* a four-hand piano work of great emotional power. He wrote to a friend towards the end of the year 'I must humbly admit to the feeling of latent death within me. Accordingly, I write like a madman or like one condemned to die the next morning.'

By December 1915 an operation was deemed necessary, and although it was successful, the doctors discovered that the cancer was now irreversible. Debussy spent most of 1916 recuperating, and struggling to complete his *Violin Sonata.* This elegiac, bittersweet work, finished by the end of summer, was to be his last. During 1917 he found the effort of composition too much, and

contented himself with finishing the libretto to his projected Poe opera. The music was never written. That October, he wrote: 'Music has completely abandoned me.'

'Papa is dead'

By January 1918 he was confined to bed. On the 25th of March he died in his Paris apartment, at the height of the last great German bombardment of the city. In a moving letter sent to her half-brother Raoul Bardac, Debussy's twelve-year-old daughter summed up the family's feelings of loss:

'... sweetly, angelically, he went to sleep for ever. What happens afterwards I cannot tell you. I wanted to burst into a torrent of tears but I repressed them because of Mama ... At the cemetery Mama of course could not hide her feelings. As for myself, I thought of nothing but one thing: 'You mustn't cry because of Mama.' And I gathered up all my courage which came – from where? I don't know. I didn't shed a tear: tears repressed are worth tears shed, and now it is to be night for ever. Papa is dead.'

To the sound of German guns rumbling in the background, and in the presence of a handful of mourners, Debussy was buried at the cemetery of Père-Lachaise in Paris on 28 March 1918.

The première of Debussy's opera, Pelléas et Mélisande in 1902 (Mélisande from a 1908 production shown left) marked a watershed in his career. It was Debussy's only opera but with it he won fame and wider recognition.

Debussy (below) with his daughter Claude-Emma (Chou-Chou) in 1916, just two years before his death.

Orchestral works

Sensuous and colourful, Debussy's orchestral music appeals to the imagination as well as the ear. Both La Mer *and* Nocturnes *are paintings in sound – the former evoking the beauty and power of the sea.*

Around the time of Debussy's birth in 1862 music in France was firmly cast in two different moulds. The spectacular, grand style of the German-born Meyerbeer and the light-hearted opera-comique of Offenbach dominated the opera house in particular and set the tone of French music in general. Outside the opera house the musical establishment was dominated by Saint-Saëns – who found his inspiration in the formal wit and elegance of the classical masters, such as Mozart, Beethoven and Mendelssohn – and by Saint-Saëns' pupil, Gabriel Fauré. The music of Berlioz, with

its highly original red-blooded Romanticism, had established few roots in his native France.

As the century progressed, however, two factors emerged which helped break the moulds and pointed French music in a new direction. The first was the impact of Wagner, whose hugely expanded musical language and lofty artistic aims helped fire the French composer Cesar Franck – and Franck, in turn, was to greatly influence his generation. The second factor was France's humiliating defeat in the Franco-Prussian war of 1870, one result of which was to

cause a reaction against German influence in the arts. This, allied to the revolutions taking place in French art and literature, promoted a reawakening of French national consciousness and set the background against which Debussy was to grow.

Debussy's early responsiveness to what was happening around him quickly showed, though the full effects on his music would not be heard until very near the end of the century. But even by the mid-1880s, just as he was beginning to compose in earnest, the influence of the Impressionist painters on his music is clearly apparent. Their brilliant use of colour, their fascination with the effects of light and atmosphere and their attempts to portray the fleeting moment all have parallels in his work – particularly in that written for orchestra.

Another, and stronger, influence on Debussy was the work of the symbolist poets. While great literature – especially the works of Shakespeare, Dante and Goethe – had played an important role in forming the ideas of the Romantic composers, not until the writings of Mallarmé

and Baudelaire appeared did it become clear, especially to Debussy, that modern poetry had something to offer music.

Debussy's style continues to influence composers profoundly, proving his success in reworking and freeing the basic materials of music to express new images and ideas. Many of the radical innovations of 20th-century music build on his pioneering work. He re-examined the constituents of music — melody, harmony, rhythm, timbre — and expanded their expressive range.

To create many of his melodies, for example, he turned to the medieval *modes,* with their strangely angular scales that are neither major nor minor; he also discovered, in the folk music of the East, rich and ornamental melodic possibilities based on pentatonic (five-note) scales and on the six-note whole-tone scale. Harmony, too, he approached in a new way. Traditional Western harmony is very hierarchical; some degrees of the scale are more important than others; tension and expression are built on carefully-prepared

In La Mer *Debussy depicts the ever-changing moods and character of the sea (below), using the 'colours' of the orchestra to conjure up a picture in sound.*

By permission of the British Library

The cover of the first edition of La Mer *(left) was illustrated with an adaptation of* The Hollow of the Wave off Kanagawa *by the Japanese artist Hokusai, whose work Debussy greatly admired.*

discords that have to be resolved. But, to support his unorthodox melodies, Debussy often used chords traditionally regarded as discords, without preparation or resolution, justifying their use purely by their beauty of sound.

Debussy's attitude to the orchestra goes hand-in-hand with his feelings about harmony. He revels in the endless possibilities of sonority, and in order to exploit these possibilities he looked afresh at the whole art of orchestration. In contrast to Wagner's lush, dense sonorities, Debussy fragmented his orchestral palette as far as possible, creating a cleanness and luminosity of sound with great economy of instrumentation.

He also rethought the normal roles assigned to each section of the orchestra — woodwind, brass, strings, percussion — allowing it as a whole to explore a far greater range. The woodwind is especially well served, with both solo and group parts — the latter written with the same precision and freedom of line as chamber music. The strings, the heart of the orchestra, have an unprecedented transparency of texture, achieved by the closest attention to divisions in part-writing and to the details of performance instructions and bowing indications. Debussy also elevated the harp to a position of independence from which it has never looked back.

All this allowed Debussy to create the *exact* sound he wanted to hear — the sound that most closely resembled whatever was the source of his inspiration. Consequently, the end always justified the means, regardless of convention. 'My music has no other aim', he wrote, 'than to melt in the minds of predisposed people and to become identified with certain scenes or objects.' That nature provided the scenes central to

Debussy's inspiration can be seen from the titles of many of his works – for example, 'Gardens in the Rain', 'Fog' and 'Moonlight'. Above all though, it was water that fascinated him most – its ever-changing face, colour, mood and character providing constantly new sources of inspiration. Thus, water recurs again and again in Debussy's work, but nowhere does he portray it better than in *La Mer* (The Sea).

La Mer

La Mer finds its pictorial inspiration in the seascapes of Turner – 'the greatest creator of mysterious effects', said Debussy, 'in the whole world of art' – and in the prints of the Japanese artists Hokusai and Hiroshige. Indeed it was *The hollow of the wave off Kanagawa* by Hokusai that Debussy chose to be reproduced on the cover of the first edition of *La Mer*. Although strongly characterized by Impressionist influences, the music's brilliant, crystalline orchestration and the firm structure of the two outer movements, with their robust, strongly-drawn themes, are the antithesis of the hazy quality so often associated with this style.

The first performance took place in October 1905, in an atmosphere of bitter feelings aroused by the circumstances surrounding Debussy's second marriage. 'The work was awaited in Paris with an impatience that was not kindly disposed', wrote Louis Laloy, '. . . on all sides people were ready to make the artist pay dearly for the wrongs that were imputed to the man.' The editor of *Monde Musical* described *La Mer* as a 'regular salad of sonorities' and claimed that one hearer had cried, 'I feel seasick!' By contrast, the music critic of *Le Temps* objected that the work was only a pallid reproduction of nature: 'I neither hear, nor see, nor feel the sea.'

Against such astonishing insensitivity, a few critics did respond to the music's power. For example, the critic of the *Mercure de France* reported: 'there are pages where one seems to tread the edges of an abyss and gaze into limitless depths . . .'

About a year after he had completed *La Mer,* Debussy wrote to his publisher: 'Here I am again with my old friend, the sea; it is always endless and beautiful. It is really the thing in Nature which restores one best to one's place.

La Mer **with its luminous, atmospheric and shimmering orchestral effects seems to find an exact counterpart in Turner's** View from Deal **(right). Debussy, in fact, admired Turner's work and called him 'the greatest creator of mysterious effects in the whole world of art'.**

Programme notes

La Mer is not only the most striking of all music evocations of the sea – but also arguably the most succesful French symphony. Debussy called it 'three symphonic sketches', and its symphonic quality is evident in the contrasting of themes as part of a development and the use of *motifs* as a strong unifying element.

'De l'aube a midi sur la mer'

The introduction to this first movement ('From dawn to midday at sea') depicts the first shafts of light softening the darkness of the gently-moving waters. Quiet *tremolandi* over the whole range of the strings suggest the huge expanses of sea and sky, through which sounds a lonely call on trumpet and cor anglais (English horn, similar to the oboe). Gradually, the music gathers momentum, leading into a section marked *Modéré, sans lenteur* (Moderate, without slowness) with a strongly-defined melody in horns against limpid figures on strings and woodwind suggesting the sea's continuous motion and the playful splash of the waves.

Example 1

The tempo relaxes into brief lyrical episodes with solo oboe and violin,

the air for a cor anglais melody supported by a chattering woodwind and string accompaniment, followed by successive lyrical solos on violin, oboe and cello which create a kaleidoscopic display of light and motion. Two powerful chords herald the return to the urgent violin melody, played now on flutes. The tension builds up over a deep sustained note and is released in a *fortissimo* eruption of great energy. Again we hear the harp *glissandi* and scraps of past melodies as the music quickly subsides into a mood of great serenity. Throughout the movement the impression of the sea's boundless activity is evoked in sounds that hover on the brink of abstraction, but the free rondo form and the deftness of melody and orchestration are just enough to hold the music together.

Dialogue du vent et de la mer

The abstract quality at the end of the second movement is given more substance in the third sketch ('Dialogue of the wind and the sea'). The opening figure on cellos and double basses represents the water's choppy surface, agitated by the sighing chords on woodwind. The excitement quickens with repeated string chords from which emerges a trumpet call, derived from the first movement. The waves become more violent, and the wind's motif grows into a defined tune:

Example 2

Bassoons and cellos take over the trumpet call, accompanied by a lithe string *ostinato*, also previously heard in the first movement. The music accelerates to a great climax, which quickly subsides, leaving a solo cornet, stranded high above an ominous chord on tuba and timpani to bring in the long closing section, which is announced by the solemn brass chorale of the first movement with shimmering string accompaniment. The wind's motif — here transfigured into a long melodic strand of benign power and later interwoven with the restless trumpet call — makes up most of the substance of the coda, finally combining with the chorale in music of breathtaking grandeur.

Nocturnes

In 1892 Debussy wrote that he had almost finished a new work which he intended to include on a projected tour of the United States. It was called *Trois scènes au crépuscule* ('Three scenes at twilight') and is believed — the score is lost — to be Debussy's first step towards creating *Nocturnes*. Two years later Debussy wrote to the violinist Eugène Ysaÿe that he was

followed by solo flute, but a strident trumpet call reflects the light's growing intensity as the music moves into the second section. This opens with a vigorous theme for the cellos. Rushing violin scales lead to a rhythmic *ostinato* (a short figure repeated again and again) of great energy in the strings; an expressive melody for cor anglais and two cellos prepares the way for the coda, a majestic brass chorale that suggests the awesome depth and super-human power of the sea sparkling in the full light of day.

Jeux de vagues

The second movement ('Play of the waves') is reminiscent of a symphonic *scherzo*. In contrast to the two outer movements, with their sharply-delineated sections, it consists of a rapid, mosaic-like succession of fleeting events that capture for an instant the effect of light on the waves. The main theme, first heard on cor anglais, produces many tendril-like arabesques, which quickly evaporate in cello trills that lead to an urgent violin melody in E major. Harp *glissandi* clear

working on three nocturnes for violin and orchestra, describing it as 'an experiment with the different combinations that can be obtained from one colour – like a study of grey in painting.' In the following few years Debussy either reworked or composed afresh the *Nocturnes* in the version known today. Debussy himself wrote of *Nocturnes:*

The title Nocturnes is to be interpreted here in a general and, more particularly, in a decorative sense. Therefore it is not meant to designate the usual form of the nocturne (as composed by Chopin), but rather all the various impressions and the special effects of light that the word suggests. 'Nuages' renders the immutable aspect of the sky and the slow, solemn motion of the clouds, fading away in grey tones lightly tinged with white. 'Fêtes' gives us the vibrating atmosphere with sudden flashes of light . . . There is also the episode of the procession (a dazzling, fantastic vision) which passes through the festive scene and becomes merged in it. But the background remains persistently the same: the festival, with its blending of music and luminous dust, participating in the cosmic rhythm. 'Sirènes' depicts the sea and its countless rhythms and presently, amongst the waves silvered by moonlight, is heard the mysterious song of the Sirens as they laugh and pass on.

Nocturnes was very well received on its

Understanding music: Impressionism in music

The emergence of the Impressionist painters in Paris was followed within a few years by that of Claude Debussy – a composer who, with Wagner, was to become one of the most influential composers on succeeding generations. Debussy himself, preferred the company of artists to that of his fellow musicians, and it was inevitable that his music, with its washes of sound created from a rich use of instrumental timbre and tone-colour, should also be described as Impressionist.

But while the Impressionist painters departed radically from the established traditions of their day – creating an entirely new approach, using new techniques, Debussy's style resulted much more directly from historical progress. The shimmering piano cascades of Liszt's *Jeux d'eaux à la villa d'Este* (Fountains at the Villa d'Este), the rich orchestral colouring of Rimsky-Korsakov's opera, *Sadko* and Wagner's epic representation of the waters of the Rhine at the beginning of *Das Rheingold* are all early examples of Impressionism in music.

Many of the features of Impressionist music are also found in the music of the various nationalist composers, and especially those whose native traditions embraced oriental elements. Scales other than the familiar major and minor – such as

pentatonic scales based on just five notes, and whole-tone scales which use six equal intervals – were used by Slav composers including Rimsky-Korsakov, Mussorgsky and Dvořák. They also tended to write music in short phrases, usually just two bars long.

This use of short phrases is particularly important as it not only created colourful sound effects by repeating and building up short patterns of notes, but because it affected the whole structure of the music. When composers turned to their native folk-traditions for inspiration, they found the short, often repeated, phrases incompatible with the traditional sonata form and sought new kinds of structures for their music. Debussy's works are no less organised than Beethoven's or Mozart's, but they are built on a different framework, using repetition of ideas, often infinitely varied like the changing patterns of a kaleidoscope, rather than the development and re-statement of contrasting themes which formed the backbone of the classical tradition. It is perhaps because of this departure from tradition that the Impressionist style of Debussy and his contemporaries was never really taken up by the Germanic composers, although his influence was widely felt in other European countries, especially England.

first complete performance in 1901. The composer Paul Dukas, who had studied with Debussy at the Conservatoire, observed that the music recalled the 'strange, delicate, vibrating Nocturnes of Whistler (a series of paintings of twilight scenes), and like the canvases of the great American painter, they are full of a deep and poignant poetry.' And the music critic of the newspaper *La Liberté* described the composer of *Nocturnes* as 'one of the most original artists of the day . . .. Guided by a refined and unerring taste, he knows how to combine harmonies and timbres in ever-changing ratios.'

Programme notes

Nuages

The first piece, *Nuages* (Clouds), grows out of two elements: the monotonous winding figure on woodwind heard at the very opening, and the short tag of melody for cor anglais, which Debussy said was inspired by the mournful sound of a boat's signal horn on the river Seine. The first element, soon taken up by the strings, is like a backdrop, evoking the gentle shifting of grey clouds; the sense of isolation and timelessness is highlighted by the haunting sound of the cor anglais. With both figures

The first movement of Debussy's Nocturnes, Nuages *(clouds), suggests the gentle shifting of grey clouds across an isolated and timeless landscape (left).*

In striking contrast to Nuages, Fêtes *uses vivid orchestral colours to portray a festival or parade in full swing (right).*

Although Debussy remained the greatest exponent of the Impressionist style, many other composers followed in his wake. In France, Ravel, while retaining a closer connection with the Classical style, wrote a number of Impressionistic works, among them the ballet *Daphnis et Chlóe* and the piano suite *Gaspard de la nuit*. The influence of Impressionism reached English composers through France – the young Vaughan Williams spent a short period of study with Ravel, while Delius, although today regarded as an English composer, actually spent most of his life in France. Their music, though quite distinctive, is highly atmospheric and evocative – a hallmark of the Impressionist style – as in Vaughan Williams' *London* symphony.

As Impressionism in art was succeeded by more radical styles, new directions were also being opened up in music. Before Debussy's death, yet another French scandal had been created by the première of Stravinsky's *The Rite of Spring,* while in Vienna, Schoenberg and his school were finally breaking the bonds of tonality and establishing new techniques of composing. Traces of Impressionism were to remain for several decades but, in Paris at least, the days of the quintessentially Impressionist work – Debussy's *Prelude à l'apres midi d'un faune* – were over.

established, there is a short passage built over violas and cellos in unison which acts as a bridge to a repeat of the cor anglais solo, but with the cloud pattern enlivened by a gentle, rhythmic pizzicato, supported by a long pedal note on double basses. The middle section starts with a lyrical flute and harp solo which is taken over by solo violin, viola and cello. This pale shaft of colour is short-lived, and the cor anglais announces the coda, which, like a cloud, disintegrates; the process is simply and hauntingly evoked by the fragmentation of the cloud theme, and with a wistful backward glance at the lyrical flute solo, the music fades into silence.

Fêtes

The second piece, *Fêtes,* is in complete contrast to the first; over a buoyant, tarantella rhythm in the strings, the woodwinds play with a strong and sinuous melody that pervades the entire movement. The brightness of colour is accentuated by woodwind, brass and strings being played off against each other; some of the orchestration – the chattering woodwind in particular – is very reminiscent of Tchaikovsky. The music builds to a climax, then abruptly changes tack to a new key and an insistent march rhythm on timpani. Fanfares are heard on muted brass, which gather in force as a procession draws nearer, erupting with powerful brilliance in full orchestra. As the parade is absorbed into the general merriment, music from the first section reappears. Finally, like *Nuages, Fêtes* evaporates.

Sirènes

One of the last of the fragments from *Fêtes* is a falling figure of two notes *(appoggiatura),* which is carried over into the last movement, *Sirènes* (Sirens), and becomes the cell from which *Sirènes* grows. *Fêtes* ends in the key of A; the opening of *Sirènes* is in F sharp, and this downward slip of three notes has the effect of the music's settling to new depths. *Sirènes* is one of the most evocative of Debussy's sea pictures and develops from the slenderest of means. There is hardly any thematic development – only the gentle assertion of the falling two-note figure, first heard on the horns and echoed by the chorus of eight sopranos and eight mezzo-sopranos, which, once it has established itself, acquires the confidence to expand, given substance by delicate arabesques on harp and woodwind and a shimmering string accompaniment. At its most extended, the sirens' song only embraces four more pitches:

Example 3

The orchestration, however, becomes increasingly more complex, suggesting the play of moonlight on the waves. The middle section is like a development, with

In Sirènes women's voices sing a haunting, seductive song evoking the legendary call of the sirens, mythical female creatures who lured sailors to their deaths (left).

The opening bars of Sirènes (shown in an early printed score, below) which include the falling, two-note song of the sirens, exemplify Debussy's effective use of sparse orchestration to create an impression of distance and mystery.

Great interpreters

Cleveland Symphony Orchestra

The orchestra was founded in Cleveland, USA, in 1918 by Adella P. Hughes, with the support of the Cleveland Musical Arts Association. The European-born Nikolai Sokoloff was its first conductor and held the post until 1933, when Artur Rodzinski took over as Musical Director.

Artur Rodzinski stayed with the orchestra for 10 years, broadening and developing its repertoire, and was succeeded by Erich Leinsdorf, who held the top post for just three years. In 1946 the Cleveland's era as one of the world's great orchestras dawned with the arrival of the brilliant and intensely disciplined George Szell. Szell demanded, and got, total response from his players and forced the standards up to such a level that within ten years the Cleveland was in the first rank of American orchestras and had a substantial reputation overseas – a reputation that was enhanced by many fine recordings.

Szell stayed until 1970, the year of his death. It was two years before a successor was appointed; this was Lorin Maazel, whose appointment was for ten years. In that time, Maazel continued to uphold the tradition of excellence, and led the orchestra into a more diverse repertoire than it had offered under Szell.

Lorin Maazel (conductor)

Maazel was born in France in 1930 but was taken to the United States as an infant and brought up in Los Angeles and Pittsburgh. As a small child he studied violin and piano, and he made his debut as a conductor at the age of seven. In 1939, aged nine, he conducted the New York Philharmonic at the World's Fair.

An extraordinary career as a prodigy developed from these beginnings. His conducting of the NBC Symphony in 1941 even won the approval of that orchestra's own conductor, Toscanini. By the end of World War II Maazel had conducted virtually every top US orchestra, while at the same time concentrating on his career as a violinist. In 1945 he gave his debut violin recital, and in the same year, still only 15, he became the leader of the Pittsburgh Fine Arts Quartet. An association with the Pittsburgh Symphony began in 1948, when he joined the orchestra as a violinist; the following year he became its assistant conductor.

Throughout the 1950s he made numerous appearances all round the world as a guest conductor, making his London debut, with the BBC Symphony, in 1960. During the 1960s he continued to gain attention and respect as a mature conductor with established companies. In 1962 he toured with L'Orchestre Nationale de Paris and made his debut at the Metropolitan Opera. In 1969 he won his first major appointments: as Artistic Director of the Deutsche Oper, West Berlin, and as Music Director of the Berlin Radio Symphony Orchestra.

Following these appointments, Maazel continued to appear as a guest conductor regularly all over the world, though devoting most of his considerable energies to Berlin. His horizons continued to broaden, however, and in 1970 he became Associate Principal Conductor of London's Philharmonia Orchestra for two years before returning to the US to accept an appointment as successor to the great George Szell with the Cleveland Symphony Orchestra.

The Cleveland appointment was for ten years, and during that time Maazel emerged as one of the top conductors of the modern concert circuit, recording successfully in both the concert and opera repertoires. Maazel was also instrumental in changing the Cleveland Orchestra's basic repertoire and extending it in many directions.

In 1981 Maazel accepted an appointment as Musical Director of the Vienna Opera, a position to which he brought all his customary energy, erudition and dedication. His incumbency in fact proved an exceptionally stormy one – not so unusual in that traditionally musically partisan city – and he resigned amid controversy in 1984 well before his contracted time. Since then he has continued to make recordings with Deutsche Gramaphonen and other companies.

Decca International

---

snatches of the sirens' song – reduced now to two pitches, but keeping the rhythmic outline – passed around the orchestra. A brief trumpet scale heralds the return of the opening, reached after a link passage that restores the sirens' song in full. The reprise summons up a wealth of luminous writing for the whole orchestra, with the song fading in and out of delicate harp arpeggios and woodwind scoring of *pointilliste* detail and with the strings divided into as many as 13 parts, bathing everything in a silvery translucence. Just before the end the music melts imperceptibly into a chord of B major.

Nocturnes is a miracle of orchestral detail. The choral writing is dovetailed to produce a seamless flow of sound that seems to require no breathing spaces and is orchestral rather than vocal in effect. Debussy makes great use of the threshold between silence and scarcely audible sound to achieve an uncannily subtle range of dynamics and timbre.

FURTHER LISTENING

Prélude à l'Après-midi d'un Faune

With this work Debussy ushered in a new era of music: the rarefied sonorities, the dreamlike atmosphere and the reliance on beautiful melody, although often employed by composers in the past, had never before served as the substance of a complete orchestral work. The piece has all the hallmarks of the mature Debussy, such as the quicksilver, elusive melodies carried by the flute and oboe against the shimmering string backdrop, and the virtual suspension of any stated beat. It is a beautifully-wrought composition, perfect of its kind.

Preludes, Books 1 and 2

These two books of 12 piano preludes each, written in his full maturity, demonstrate his search for accurate portrayals of intimate feelings and recollections, or of only dimly-

perceived sensations. Each title (for example, 'Footsteps in the Snow', 'The Maid with Flaxen Hair') suggests the mood or image evoked by the music. Among his subjects are dead leaves, and the scent and sound of the evening air. Debussy paints a broad canvas, from sly and rollicking humour to refined mystery and spectacular brilliance, in this exquisite collection of pieces.

Trois Chansons de Bilitis

These three songs are settings of poems by Pierre Louÿs, and are mercurial, dazzling musical evocations of the sentiments, yearnings and passions expressed by the young girl who is the narrator of these lyrics. Debussy's remarkable sensitivity to the sounds and inner rhythms of words and syntax is triumphantly demonstrated in each of these three songs.

'Anarchists and madmen'

French painting was thrust forward into the 20th century by the twin forces of Impressionism and Symbolism – and the reverberations shook the artistic world from literature to music.

The French 'Impressionist' painters of the late 19th century are among the most popular of all artists nowadays, and prints of paintings by the core of the group – Renoir, Monet, Pissarro and Sisley – adorn the walls of houses right across the world. The shimmering colours, the glorious sense of light, the simple, natural choice of subject and, above all, their tremendous zest for life give Impressionist paintings a charm and appeal that captivates even those with only a passing interest in art. And their major role in the development of modern art is now fully established – so established that they are sometimes dismissed as 'too safe'.

Yet in the 1870s, the revolutionary techniques and approach of the Impressionists were too much for the art establishment and public alike, and they were

It was this painting (right) by Claude Monet, called Impression, Sunrise, *that gave the Impressionists their name. The art critic Louis Leroy coined the word in his mocking review of the 1874 exhibition, intending it to convey the artists' 'sloppy' approach. The name stuck.*

An early champion of the Impressionists was the writer and critic Émile Zola (left), but he was out-spoken in his support.

Such was the furore created by the Impressionists' first exhibition that one can almost believe this satirical cartoon by Cham (left). It shows how the Turks might buy many impressionist paintings to use as weapons against their enemies, so terrible were they.

villified and scorned for many years. Indeed, the idea of the struggling artist, starving for his art, his talent unrecognized, was fostered to a great extent by the trials and tribulations of the Impressionist painters. The winding streets of Montmartre in Paris may now seem a chic and picturesque artist's quarter, but for some of the painters who established its reputation, it was simply the only place they could afford to live. Even in 1894, 20 years after the first Impressionist exhibition, the bequest of 67 Impressionist paintings to the Louvre by the painter Gustave Caillebotte aroused enormous hostility and official embarassment. Typically, one member of the academic establishment ranted:

Only great moral depravity could bring the State to accept such rubbish. These artists are all anarchists and madmen!

One of the most shocking features of Impressionism was its apparent carelessness of execution. Paint seemed to be just slopped onto the canvas with no real attempt to draw the shapes clearly, no attempt to reproduce textures and forms accurately, and the pictures appeared to be merely rough sketches, not finished works of art – even the crude brush strokes were clearly visible. Indeed, there was no evidence of any of the traditional painterly skills at all.

Worse still, for the art establishment, was the thoughtlessness of it all. Instead of the established subjects worthy of artistic study, the Impressionists simply painted scenes from everyday life, scenes that anyone could see, at any time. Renoir painted people in the cafes of Montmartre; Sisley painted suburban street scenes. And there was no attempt to compose these scenes within the picture frame in the time-honoured manner. They were fleeting glimpses, moments caught not arranged. In Renoir's paintings, arms, legs, even faces disappear beyond the edge of the frame. Although candid photographic snapshots have made us familiar with such images, they seemed bizarre to people in the 1870s. Only recently has Renoir's true mastery of composition been appreciated. To cap it all, there was no message in the pictures. They had nothing to say; they just existed. No wonder the Impressionists appeared to have no talent at all and to some seemed to be frauds.

Oddly enough, all these individual criticisms had at least some foundation in truth, particularly amongst the less capable Impressionist painters, and it may be that this was why they found it so hard to gain recognition. But the critics completely missed the point, failing to understand what the Impressionists were trying to do.

When Monet painted *Impression, Sunrise* in 1872, he was trying to capture as accurately as possible the real visual effect of a misty morning sun upon water – the way he actually saw the interplay of light and colour, not an interpretation of the scene that revealed each object. Monet's advice to painters gives a clear indication of his approach.

Try to forget what objects you have before you – a tree, a house, a field or whatever. Merely think, here, is a little square of blue, here an oblong of pink, the exact colour and shape, until it gives your own naive impression of the scene before you.

The word 'naive' is important, for Monet believed, along with the other Impressionists, that it was essential to approach the subject with a completely fresh, open mind, rid of preconception of what the scene should look like. Only this way could you be totally objective.

For the Impressionists, capturing the rapid changes of light and colour in the atmosphere, rather than telling a story, was the central aim of their art. To achieve it, they evolved a revolutionary method of painting on the spot with rapid brush strokes – for it would be impossible to sketch these subtle atmospheric effects in pencil and then recall them in the studio.

They combined this location painting method with a new way of building up colour that drew its

Claude Monet was, with Renoir, one of the two giants of Impressionism and this painting Coin de Jardin à Montgeron *(right) is typical of his work. It was of Monet that Paul Cézanne later said, 'he was only an eye – but, my god, what an eye!' and this painting, with its shimmering interplay of light and colour, shows that eye to marvellous effect. The picture is built up with short deft brush strokes of pure colour.*

The Entrée du village de Voisins *(below left) is one of Camille Pissarro's contributions to the 1874 exhibiton – Pissarro was the only painter to contribute to all eight Impressionist exhibitions – and owes much to the influence of Corot.*

Auguste Renoir's À la Grenouillère *(below right) shows one of his favourite subjects, a healthy young woman in a natural everyday pose – the kind of subject and pose that was unheard of before the days of Impressionism.*

inspiration from recent discoveries on the way the eye sees colours. One of these discoveries was that the eye tends to see in shadows not simply a darker version of the subject colour, but its complementary colour – so shadows could be filled with all kinds of different colours. Another even more important discovery was that colour is not an inherent quality of objects, but simply the way the eye mixes light reflected from it. So there was no need to paint an object in its 'true' colour, you could build up its colour from a series of different, pure colour brush strokes. The eye would cause these colours to give an impression of the 'true' colour. The result, it was believed, would be both more vibrant and more realistic.

The origins of Impressionism

In many ways, Impressionism marks the logical and final development of a search that had been going on from the early 19th century, both in England and in France, to find a more truthful way of representing Nature. Throughout the previous century, French art had been dominated by the idea that only historical, religious or classical subjects were worth painting. This idea gained weight through the powerful institution of the French Academy of Fine Arts and its bi-annual official exhibitions in the *salon carré* of the

Monet 'Corner of the Garden at Montgeron'. Hermitage, Leningrad/Mauro Pucciarelli-Roma © DACS 1990

air rather than from the comfort of their studios, these artists set a powerful precedent for the Impressionists.

Yet despite this burgeoning of realistic landscape painting among the younger artists, the Salon still tended to feature the traditional subjects almost exclusively. Naturally this caused deep resentment, for the Salon had a crucial impact on public taste and sales of pictures. It came to a head in 1855, when some of Gustave Courbet's paintings were refused for the Salon at the Paris exhibition.

Courbet was the most influential of the younger painters and, although distanced from the Barbizon school, believed painting was the 'representation of real and existing objects'. He wanted to paint village funerals, stonebreakers and country people, not the traditional subjects. Faced with rejection by the Salon, Courbet staged his own rival exhibition called the 'Pavilion of Realism'. The impact of Courbet's fresh, bold paintings alongside the tired old works that hung in the Salon was remarkable. Courbet's exhibition set an important precedent which the Impressionists were later to follow. More importantly, it broke forever the stranglehold of traditional academic subjects.

The growing movement

Through the gap opened by Courbet came the whole Impressionist group, fathered in the 1860s, by Edouard Manet. Where Courbet had still used conventional techniques if not subjects, Manet developed a sketchy style, using pure colour to give a very realistic look even to studio subjects. The results, in works like *Déjeuner sur l'herbe* and *Olympia,* caused a sensation. The public could not come to terms with Manet's way of painting exactly what he saw. It seemed indecently and shockingly real! Manet too was shut out of the Salon, despite being championed by the outspoken art critic (later the novelist) Emile Zola. And, in 1867, he followed Courbet's example and organized his own exhibition – one-man exhibitions are one of our most notable legacies from the Impressionist era.

Louvre and the so-called Salons.

Remarkably, both the idea and the institution survived the revolution of 1789 intact, but amongst younger artists, the romantic movement and increasing urbanization and industrialization was fostering a passion for nature and growing preference for landscapes. The Salon, however, continued to favour the traditional subjects almost exclusively.

In England, though, landscape painting already had a long history and by the early 19th century was progressing in leaps and bounds with the paintings of John Constable and J M W Turner. In 1825, Constable's *The Hay Wain* was exhibited in Paris and its fresh colours and bold sketchy technique were a tremendous inspiration to young French painters. More important still was its simple, everyday subject and natural quiet landscape.

By the late 1830s and the 1840s, many young French painters were going out into the country to paint *real* landscapes in the open air. One village called Barbizon, situated on the edge of the forest of Fontainebleau, attracted a whole string of fine landscape painters – Camille Corot, Théodore Rousseau, Jean Millet, Charles Daubigny and many others, who thus became known as the Barbizon School. Observing and studying nature in the open-

Renoir 'À la Grenouillère'. Musée d'Orsay, Paris/Garanger-Giraudon

Cézanne 'La Montagne Sainte-Victoire'. Kunsthaus, Zurich/Giraudon

Although not actually an Impressionist, Manet's anti-establishment stance made him the focus of the young group of artists who were to create the new movement. In the late 1860s, a whole group of artists would gather round Manet at the Café Guerbois in Paris to drink coffee and wine and discuss art vociferously. Among them were Degas, Monet and Renoir, Berthe Morisot and the photographer Nadar. Émile Zola was also a frequent visitor to the Café and, if he disagreed with their ideas, always resolutely defended the Impressionists. Another occasional participant was the poet Baudelaire.

It was from these sessions in the Café Guerbois that the idea for the first Impressionists exhibition emerged. For the previous decade, Monet and Renoir had worked side by side out of doors at La Grenouillère, a cafe and boating place on the Seine, and produced a series of paintings that, in their quick, definite brush strokes and informal subject matter, provided the basis for the full Impressionist style. By the early 1870s, Monet, Renoir, Sisley, Pissarro and others had developed this style to a

remarkable extent. But there was still no recognition from the establishment. So, in 1874, the group, now led by Monet and Pissarro, decided to stage their own exhibition at Nadar's studio near the elegant Boulevard des Capucines.

The exhibition, which opened on 15 April, caused a public and critical sensation. It was, in fact, one of the critics, Louis Leroy of the satirical journal *Le Charivari,* who gave the group their name. Faced with Monet's *Impression, Sunrise,* he called Monet an 'impressionist' in his mocking review to characterize his 'sloppy' style and the name stuck. Leroy went on to lament:

Oh Corot, Corot, what crimes are committed in your name! It was you who brought into fashion this messy composition, these thin washes, these mud-splashes in front of which the art lover has been rebelling for 30 years.

The Impressionists remained undaunted by the abuse and lack of understanding, even if their material circumstances remained straightened. And

Despite the almost abstract style of some of his later work, Cézanne always painted his landscapes in the open air. One of his favourite views was of Mont Ste Victoire and the painting above is just one of a celebrated series he painted of the mountain. This re-working of the same subject was important as, although like the Impressionists Cezanne drew from nature, he painted not his first impression but a studied view.

they continued to develop their style. During the late 1870s, with Monet and Renoir working together at Argenteuil, Pissarro not far away at Pointoise and Sisley at Port Marly, some of the most characteristic examples of Impressionist painting appeared. Soon each artist found his own favourite subject. For Monet, water, with its continually changing reflections of light and colour, was especially attractive. Similarly, the myriad reflections from snow held a special fascination for Sisley. Renoir, after working with Monet on water and landscape themes found his challenge in the constant bustle of the boulevards of Paris and its cafes.

A dead end

Ironically, it was the very concern with the way the light and colour changed that proved to be the main reason for the short life of Impressionism – barely a decade. By 1880, the Impressionists and some of their followers had begun to sense that their treatment of light and colour did not tell the full story. More to the point, they began to feel, along with many others, that the search for complete realism was fruitless. The pursuit of realism, which had been going on since the Renaissance, seemed to have no further to go – painting reality was ultimately meaningless and the reaction to the most real imaginable picture could be 'So what?'

The problem was where to go. The Impressionists were not alone in their search. Realism, and its successor Naturalism, had played a significant part in all art forms at the time and was now beginning to ask the same questions. Influenced by the German philosophers, Schopenhauer, Hegel and Nietzsche, artists began to fall more in line with a new movement called 'Symbolism' which wanted art to contain imaginative, spiritual and sensual ideas, conveyed in symbolic terms. There was also an increasing concern with dreams and allegorical visions – it is perhaps significant that it was at this time that Freud's first discoveries about dreams, symbols and the importance of sex were being made.

Not every artist followed the Symbolist line and, in painting, the urge towards imaginative expression took two main directions forward from Impressionism: that of Monet, Cézanne and Seurat who developed a kind of Post-Impressionism (Seurat's version was called 'Neo-Impressionism'), eventually transforming the Impressionist search for 'Truth to Nature' into an art based on the personal contemplation of nature: and that of the Synthestists and Symbolists like Gauguin and Van Gogh, Moreau and Puvis de Chavannes, who tried to explore themes of intensely personal symbols. The oddity is that though working from such totally different directions, the common ground that formed their point of departure, the discovery of colour, led in the end to paintings that in many ways were surprisingly similar. Between them these paintings were to revolutionize art in the early 20th century.

Post-Impressionism

Of the original group of Impressionists, Monet found the only truly successful and consistent style in the years after 1880. His solution was to paint a series of pictures on exactly the same subject, seen at different times of the day and under different atmospheric conditions. There were first the 15 paintings of *Haystacks* in 1891, followed by six views of *Poplars on the River Epte* in 1891 and 1892, and then some twenty views of the facade of Rouen Cathedral.

But the ultimate and most astonishing develop-

Paul Gauguin's Vision after the Sermon *(right) painted in 1886 was his first great masterpiece in his 'new style'. In many ways, it was one of the first great 'Symbolist' works. The picture shows the people of a Breton village recalling a sermon about Jacob wrestling with the angels, but it is neither visionary nor 'realistic'. Instead, it uses pure vivid colours like red, flat shapes and fluid outlines to create a new expressive form of art, a form that was to lead forward to the abstract art of the 20th century.*

Gauguin 'The Vision After the Sermon' National Gallery of Scotland, Edinburgh

ment of these ideas in Monet's art are the works that occupied him for the last 30 years of his life from 1895 onwards: the water gardens and lily ponds at his garden at Giverny. In these paintings, essentially one enormous series, Monet created a completely separate world of his own, of slowly moving water and undulating plants, with the world beyond known only by the vague reflections of sky and clouds above. Painted largely in his studio, the gardens became visions, half-seen, half-remembered in the mind's eye, the colour and brushstrokes being freed almost totally from the objects themselves in a way that, at times, resembles the much later techniques of 20th century Abstract Impressionism.

A similar change of direction overtook the work of Paul Cézanne. Of the same generation as the Impressionists, he had been very much slower to find his direction and never evolved a truly Impressionist style. By 1880 he had already become dissatisfied with its results, determined instead to try and find a way of translating his visual sensations when looking at nature into strong harmonious designs, that could stand comparison with the great compositions of the Old Masters and avoid the messiness and lack of structure that he felt so weakened Impressionism. He retreated from Paris to his home in Aix-en-Provence where he lived and worked in almost total isolation, working the problem out for the next quarter of a century.

Like Monet, Cézanne found working in themes or series a helpful way of exploring these sensations, the static qualities of table-top still lifes or the Mont Ste Victoire providing fixed points against which he could return time and again to record the gradual changes in his perceptions of them. In the Mont Ste Victorie paintings of the 1890s and 1900s, he can be seen steadily reversing the Impressionist argument, as the attempt to see the world becomes an intense act of contemplation. Each picture, with its brilliant mosaic of tightly interlocking colour, stands as a symbol of his feelings when painting it. Like Monet, hard observation became transformed into a profound meditation on nature.

The last and most puzzlingly eccentric of those artists who aimed at transforming rather than breaking with Impressionism is Georges Seurat. A man of scientific and logical frame of mind, he was deeply impressed by the contemporary scientific colour theory and he felt that the Impressionist difficulties lay in the fact that they had been too casual in their treatment of light and colour. He evolved a technique which he called 'divisionism' but which is commonly referred to as 'pointillism'. It involved painting each colour as little dots of pure colour which would be mixed by the eye to give the right colour. The effect, as seen in his great outdoor masterpiece *A Sunday Afternoon on the Island of the Grand Jatte* is paradoxically far more artificial and symbolic than any Impressionist painting. The treatment has a positive almost abstract sense of form which has a poetic, timeless feel and this made the work much admired by the younger Symbolist writers and artists in the later 1880s.

Symbolism

In 1886, two younger painters, Bernard and Anquetin, made a conscious decision 'to abandon the Impressionists in order to allow Ideas to dominate the techniques of painting'. It was a decision which was to have immense significance for the new anti-art-establishment movement of the late 1880s. They wanted to find an art based on emotional experience rather than on visual analysis, a way of exploring the unconscious and instinctive parts of the mind as a source of ideas for painting. But it was Gauguin and Van Gogh who were to take this new symbolist idea into the forefront of European art. In the late 1880s, Gauguin and van Gogh both evolved a radical style in which bold, often unnaturalistic colour and strongly contoured decorative shapes were used to convey

In his 'Symbolist Manifesto' of 1886, the poet Jean Moreas had talked about the need to clothe the 'Idea' in sensual form and to reject the spirit of realism that had produced both the Impressionists and the naturalist novels of Émile Zola. His ideas, which he continued to express in the Symbolist journal (above), found an echo in the work of artists in many different fields.

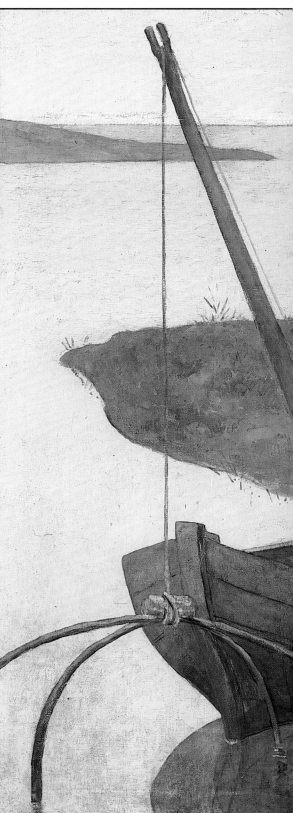

expressive and highly charged spiritual messages.

By 1888, Gauguin had, in his first great masterpiece *The Vision after the Sermon,* painted in the remote countryside of Brittany, shown the main elements of the revolutionary art he was later to develop in the South Seas. It reveals priests and peasants emerging from the church, vividly recollecting in their imaginations the sermon they had just heard about Jacob wrestling with the angels.

The peasants and their thoughts are distinguished by areas of flat, unnatural colour. Heavily influenced by Japanese art and Medieval stained glass, Gauguin's style found a way of exploiting the expressive possibilities of colour and form most effectively, building on art that was to lead to the first explorations of abstraction in the early 20th century.

The search for a still more primitive expressive power led him to Tahiti and the South Seas. There the

In the 1880s, Puvis de Chavannes was a hero among the younger symbolist painters and this painting (Le Pauvre Pêcheur) is one of his best (left). Unlike Gauguin, Puvis' background was the traditional academic style, not the avant garde of the Impressionists. By using allegory, Puvis and other painters of the older generation, like Moreau and Redon, tried to breathe new life into the traditional forms with new symbolic meanings. His paintings had a profound influence on Gauguin, but Gauguin later commented, 'Puvis explains his idea but he does not paint it.' Only now is Puvis' work being re-evaluated.

colour harmonies became richer and more exotic, the symbolism more complex, especially in its allusions to primitive versus civilized societies. In a letter from the South Seas he wrote:

Colour which is vibration just as music, reaches what is most general and therefore vaguest in nature: its interior force . . .
Here in my hut, in complete silence, I dream violent harmonies in the natural scents which intoxicate me. A delight distilled from some indescribably sacred horror which I glimpsed of far off things . . .'

Gauguin had described the creative process as 'an eruption of intense feeling which flows like lava from the depths of one's being'. But it is Van Gogh who seems to epitomize this view of the creative process. A meeting with Gauguin in Paris had confirmed Van Gogh's growing belief that 'colour expresses something in itself'. Van Gogh hoped to develop an art that through the radiance of its coloured light would create images which in their 'heartbroken expression of our times' would help others as they had helped him. Like Gauguin, Cézanne and even Monet, he had found it necessary to go and work out these ideas on his own, spending the last three violently productive years of his life in Provence. The bold colours and shapes of his paintings, their writhing lines and the agitated brushwork convey a claustrophobic and oppressive atmosphere that it is impossible to mistake. As in Gauguin and Cézanne, the progression towards an art in which feeling was symbolized by colour and design was only achieved by great suffering. In Van Gogh's art there is the added sense of living on the edge of a precipice, in which painting becomes a lifeline to human comfort, a means of personal communication that makes him the true forerunner of 20th century Expressionism. But his sense of pictorial beauty prevented his style from fragmenting into non-representational art. Only as depression, despair and madness took a grip of him did his bright colours take on an overcast menace and his landscapes verge on chaos.

The road to 20th-century art

With Van Gogh committing suicide in 1890, Seurat dying and Gauguin departing for the South Seas the following year, most of the leading avant-garde artists of the 1880s were no longer in Paris. The vacuum was mostly filled by those who had worked with Gauguin in Pont-Aven, with even younger artists impressed and influenced by his ideas. Among the former, the most significant was Paul Serusier, who as an art student had in 1888 taken lessons direct from Gauguin in Brittany. The painting deriving directly from these lessons was a tiny landscape, painted on the back of a cigar box, known as *The Talisman*. It grew into an important symbol of his ideas, ideas which Serusier and a fellow student, Maurice Denis, actively propogated. With its flat areas of unmodelled yellows, blues and greens creating a surface pattern distinct from, and in tension with, the landscape they described, *The Talisman* was a revelation, in terms of the expressive, abstract power of colours and shapes, to the next generation of artists. A small group of artists calling themselves the Nabis – Hebrew for Prophet – met to discuss these ideas and soon established themselves as the most original of the new artistic groupings. Vuillard and Bonnard are the most striking artists of the group, their fascination with pattern and surface

composition being used to describe scenes from Parisian daily life. Vuillard's preoccupation was with people in interiors, like *Misa at the Piano and Cipa Listening,* where patterns of wall-paper, textiles and lamplight transform everyday experience into a subtle and ambiguous poetry. They are introverted pictures, showing people within their own environment. Bonnard by comparison is much more extrovert and out of doors as the witty painting of *Two Dogs Playing* shows, though the decorative patterning effect is very similar.

Taken together, therefore, the discoveries of Monet, Seurat, Cezanne, Gauguin and Van Gogh and the Nabis' own clear advances towards abstraction, all led inevitably forwards to 20th century Modernism – and Impressionism and Symbolism had done much to point the way.

In the swelling tide of rejection of realist and Impressionist art, the Symbolist Gustave Moreau suddenly found his mystical, sensual paintings highly fashionable. His painting of 'The Siren' (below) is typical of his decadent, dreamy interpretations of mythical figures.

THE GREAT COMPOSERS

Maurice Ravel

1875–1937

Born in France of Swiss-Basque parents, Maurice Ravel looked to his Basque roots to provide inspiration for the greatest of his works. As a student at the Paris Conservatoire, the young Ravel's desire to keep abreast of his musical and literary contemporaries interfered with his studies. Yet despite his failure to win the Prix de Rome, his devotion to the artistic community and his place in the 'Apaches' of Parisian cafe society placed him firmly in the camp of new composers, and he soon found public acclaim for his fresh, spontaneous style. After the interruption of World War I, he returned to composition, evoking the Spain of his own imagination in the enormously successful Bolero, analysed in the Listener's Guide. Many artists were influenced by romantic notions of Spain, as In The Background shows, but perhaps none pictured Spain so enduringly as Ravel in Bolero. Like many of his works, it was startling and extremely expressive, and helped to move music forward into the 20th century.

All his life, Maurice Ravel felt deeply drawn to the Basque and Spanish heritage of his mother; his feelings were reflected not only in his music, but also in his character. Brought up in Paris, Ravel attended the Paris Conservatoire. His desire to explore the music and literature of his contemporaries and his central position in the group of artists called the 'Apaches' helped to shape his exotic style. Ravel was a private man, much given to feeling deeply but showing no one, a characteristic he attributed to his Basque roots. A series of remarkable works and concert tours of Europe and America gave him increasing fame, and the financial security to live elegantly. After a motor accident in 1932, however, Ravel's health gradually declined; he died after an operation in 1937.

COMPOSER'S LIFE

'Never a heart'

Maurice Ravel, the impeccable, cultivated gourmet of the Parisian musical scene, helped lead French music forward into the 20th century with his smooth, precise but strikingly original compositions.

Maurice Ravel (below), on the quayside in front of the house where he was born in the French Basque town of Ciboure. All his life Ravel felt deeply drawn to the Basque and Spanish heritage of his mother, a Basque, born in the Pyrenees (right), who had spent much of her childhood in Spain.

Brought up in Paris and living nearly all his life in France, Maurice Ravel was claimed by the French wholeheartedly, and completely, as their own. But the composer himself felt his roots lay elsewhere, in the homeland of his parents.

Ravel's father's family had for many generations lived in the French Haute-Savoie, near the Swiss border, and his father Pierre-Joseph Ravel had actually been born in Switzerland. His mother Marie Deluarte, however, was Basque, from the Pyrenees, and had spent much of her childhood in Madrid. It was this Basque and Spanish heritage to which the adult Ravel felt drawn so strongly.

Indeed, Pierre-Joseph and Marie first met in Aranjuez in Spain, although they were actually married in Paris in April 1873, and Maurice, their first child, was born in Basque country, in Ciboure, on 7 March 1875. Three months later, however, the family moved permanently to Paris where Pierre-Joseph had found employment as an engineer. They settled in a small house in Montmartre where their second and last child, Edouard, was born in 1878.

The family was an unusually close one, and Maurice remained devoted to them all his life. He was closest to his mother, and his relationship with her was probably the single most important emotional attachment in his life. His adoration was amply reciprocated. Through his mother Ravel inherited a deep love of the Basque country and Spanish music and, perhaps also, the rigorous repression of outward emotions that was to characterize the mature man. This trait he proudly told friends was directly attributable to his Basque descent, for it is a Basque tradition to feel deeply but show no one.

Ravel's aptitude for music was noticed early by his father, and by the time he was seven his parents had found him his first piano teacher. Four years later, as the boy's proficiency increased, a harmony teacher was also procured. Young Maurice had a happy and carefree attitude toward life and was not a particularly diligent pupil. He was never forced by his parents to practise, but still managed to make reasonable progress. By the age of 12, he was already

trying his hand at composition, writing pieces his tutor Charles-René later described as 'works of real interest, already indicating . . . an impeccable, elevated style'.

At this time, Ravel had long hair and looked like a 'Florentine page'. In 1888, he met a Spanish boy with equally long hair, Ricardo Viñes, and the two boys were to become firm friends. Ricardo also played the piano and he and Maurice would often play music together while their mothers talked in Spanish.

Both boys passed the entrance exam to the Paris Conservatoire of Music on the same day in November 1889. They spent many illicit hours at the piano together, discovering much music outside of the Conservatoire's strict curriculum. Such tendencies in the two boys were only encouraged by

The Edison phonograph (left) was one of the many inventions displayed at the Paris International Exposition of 1889. Although Ravel must have followed the early development of sound recording in the last decades of the 19th century it was only in the late 1920s that he first committed his music to disc. He was in no doubt about the opportunities afforded by the gramophone, realizing that recording would 'constitute a real document for posterity to consult . . .'

In 1889 Ravel and his musical friends were encouraged and delighted by the exotic music – very different to their daily fare at the Conservatoire – from all around the world which they heard for the first time at the Paris International Exposition (left).

Ravel met Ricardo Viñes (above, left), when they were both young boys in 1888. Ricardo was also a pianist and in 1889 both Ravel and Viñes were admitted to the Paris Conservatoire of Music. Both found music outside the Conservatoire's strict curriculum more to their liking, and together explored new avenues in music as well as other contemporary arts.

the exotic music from all round the world showcased at the Paris Universal Exhibition. Their explorations were not restricted to music though, and they made contact with many works of contemporary Parisian artists and writers such as Baudelaire, Mallarmé and Verlaine.

In 1893, the two young musicians were taken to meet Emmanuel Chabrier, a highly original French composer and pianist. The meeting made a profound impression on Ravel, and later that year he composed Sérénade grotesque in Chabrier's style. The same year, Ravel's father introduced him to another French composer whose influence was to be even more potent, the eccentric Erik Satie. Satie at this time was a penniless and largely self-taught 27 year-old playing piano at the café Chat Noir in Montmartre. They must have made an odd pair, Satie a bizarre mixture of frock-coat, pince-nez, goatee beard and general tattiness, while Ravel even at this stage was exhibiting the extreme dandyism of dress which was to remain with him all his life. Both were small men. Indeed Ravel, even when fully grown, was hardly more than five feet. Although his body was well-proportioned, his head was a little too large for its frame; a situation Ravel was not slow to try to compensate for by growing various luxurious

stylings of facial hair before yielding to fate and remaining clean-shaven for most of his adult life.

Satie was to have an important shaping influence on Ravel, just as he did on so many French composers during his lifetime, right up to his death in 1925. For the young Ravel, his importance lay in his ability to point the way towards a new and exotic simplicity based on studies of the old Greek modes, and in strikingly unresolved harmonic progressions.

All this found its place in Ravel's music in the next few years, just as the literature he avidly devoured, that of the French Symbolists and Decadents who were his contemporaries, was to provide him with texts for his songs for years to come. In this, the composer's very real concern to keep abreast of his own age is very much in evidence.

The young composer spent six years at the Conservatoire absorbing as much as he deemed necessary from his academic mentors, while continuing to explore the music of such mavericks as Chabrier and Satie in his free time. The inevitable result was that he became lax, inattentive and irregular in his attendance. He was bored, and being a talented youth indulged by his parents, he did not hesitate to show it. Predictably enough, in 1895 he was dismissed from his harmony and piano classes;

As a young composer Maurice Ravel (right) spent six years as a student at the Paris Conservatoire, where he absorbed in a selective way what he felt was necessary to his musical development. At the same time he continued to explore the music of his contemporaries in his determination to keep abreast of his own age.

not that this was the last he was to hear of them, or they of him, for that matter.

First successes

By 1897 the erstwhile student was feeling sufficiently contrite to approach the Conservatoire for more tutoring. He was accepted into the advanced composition class given by the composer Gabriel Fauré. This, plus private study with André Gédalge, gave Ravel the finishing touches he deemed necessary for his compositional technique. An indication of his continuing interest in the exotic was the unfinished opera on the subject of Sheherazade, of which only the overture was ever performed. At the premiere of this overture, Ravel remained unmoved at the furore the work caused. A letter to his friend Florent Schmitt reveals a deep irony.

'Shéhérazade' was violently whistled at . . . D'Indy, whose attitude toward me was perfect, exulted over the fact that the public could still get excited over anything. As far as I could judge from the podium, I was satisfied with the orchestra.

This concert placed Ravel firmly in the camp of the new composers, of whom Debussy was the acknowledged leader. The critics were to remain hostile for years to come, looking in vain for what they considered would be the saving grace of a Germanic influence.

Ravel's next composition made him famous, although it did not make him rich, or alter his student status. It was the *Pavane pour une Infante défunte.* The title and the stately dance rhythm showed the composer's love of all things antique and Spanish, with its conjuring of a princess from another age.

The **Menuet antique** *for piano (title page below), the first of Ravel's compositions to be published, was dedicated to his friend Ricardo Viñes.*

Ravel later tired of the piece, especially after hearing performances of it which caused him to exclaim, 'It is the princess who is dead, not the Pavane!'

The newly-successful composer entered the next century as a man secure in his opinions, possessed of a ready wit and discerning taste, still living with his parents but with a wide circle of friends in Parisian society. Yet, remarkably, he was still a student at the Conservatoire, and in 1900 failed even to qualify for the final round of the Prix de Rome, the Conservatoire's highest honour. The following year was even worse: he failed a compulsory exam for fugue writing and so was expelled from Fauré's class as a matter of course.

This setback left no public impression. He composed his first pianistic masterpiece, *Jeux d'Eau,* in the same year (he dedicated it to Fauré, with whom he had a strong friendship despite his expulsion), and in the next couple of years continued to write startling new works. And in his private life he was as independent as ever. Asked by a rich music-lover to play piano duets with him, Ravel replied, 'as long as we play no Beethoven, no Schumann, no Wagner or any other romantic music . . . in fact, as long as we play only Mozart.'

(Albert) Mac-Nab (L'écran: Napoléon, par Caran d'Ache) Rodolphe Salis Coquelin cadet
Auguste Holmès Emat Fleuze Henri Rochefort Clovis Hugues Coquelin aîné
Juliette Adam Albert Wolff Ferdinand de Lesseps Gabriel Boulanger
Carolus Duran Reichemberg

Chat-Noir — La première des projections d'ombres de « L'Epopée » dessinées par Caran d'Ache (1886)

In 1893 Ravel met the eccentric French composer Erik Satie, whose influence on him was to be profound. Through him Ravel was introduced to the much-celebrated café society of Montmartre. Together they frequented the famous Chat Noir (above) which was also the haunt of many other artistic figures such as Emile Zola (at the centre table).

From 1898 to 1903 Ravel studied composition under the composer Gabriel Fauré (right). Although thirty years Ravel's senior, a close friendship developed between the two.

Mauro Pucciarelli-Roma

The 'Apaches'

As the early years of the century went by, Ravel's life was increasingly devoted to the artistic community which met regularly at painter Paul Sordes' house. Within a short space of time his keen intelligence and his refusal to become embroiled in petty disputes had made him the unofficial central figure of the group which in 1903, the year he returned to the Conservatoire, picked up the nickname of 'the Apaches'. This had come about through the group returning en masse from a concert, dressed outrageously (as was so often the custom for Parisian intellectuals, and especially these aesthetes) and arguing very loudly among themselves as to the relative merits of what they had just heard. A poor newspaper boy selling his wares took fright at their approach, turning and running off bellowing 'beware the Apaches!' to amazed bystanders. The group were so amused by the incident that they adopted this as their name.

It was the Apaches who in these years attended the première of Debussy's *Pelleas and Melisande,* indulged in countless soirées together, participated in the authorship row between Debussy and Ravel over a harmonic and rhythmic device both had used, and finally, in 1905, helped to bring 'l'affaire Ravel' to boiling point.

The scandal came about through Ravel's dogged pursuit of the Prix de Rome, which by this time had become more a point of honour than anything else, for the composer was already recognized in the larger world. 1905 was the last year Ravel would be eligible, for when he turned 31 the following March, he would be barred from the competition. And in 1905, the judges, headed by arch-conservative Théodore Dubois, eliminated Ravel before even the finals. Such shoddy treatment was inexcusable, and the outcry soon reverberated beyond the small circle of the Apaches and Ravel's few supporters in the establishment such as Fauré and Massenet. It spilled over into the daily papers, moving even the famed novelist Romain Rolland to write a letter of protest to the Académie des Beaux-Arts. The furore only died down with the resignation of Conservatoire Director Dubois, and the appointment of Fauré in his place.

Ravel's reaction to all this public venting of anger was typical. He refused to comment at any stage of the scandal, and, at its conclusion, accepted an invitation to go on a long cruise of Europe's rivers with two close friends. Any private relief he might have felt was concealed even from his most intimate friends. Perhaps Rolland's words had been enough,

Ravel entered the Prix de Rome not as a student, but as a composer who has already passed his examinations. I am astonished at the composers who dared judge him. Who will judge them in their turn?

Ravel saw little change in his life in the next three years. He continued to live at his parents' home in Paris, and earned little or no money from his composing. Only his father's death, after a lingering illness in 1908, disturbed this pattern. Though nothing like the blow his mother's death would be ten years later, the loss was still keenly felt, and the family turned in upon itself for support. Ravel, as usual, never mentioned it to anyone. Only the deepening emotional commitment in his works gave a clue to what he felt at this time.

A costume designed by Leon Bakst for the 1912 Ballets Russes production of Daphnis and Chloé *(above). Ravel was commissioned by the director of the Ballets Russes, Sergei Diaghilev, to write the music for the ballet.*

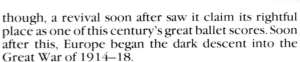
Motley Books

The Ballets Russes

The next event to impinge on his ordered and cultured existence was the arrival of Sergei Diaghilev's Ballets Russes in Paris. The troupe's sensational debut in 1909 with Mussorgsky's *Boris Godunov* had ensured that the group, then operating as both a ballet and opera company, would take Paris by storm. And of course Ravel and his group, as well as people such as the young Jean Cocteau, Picasso, Debussy and others were quickly drawn into Diaghilev's schemes and productions. But it was Diaghilev himself who introduced the then-unknown Igor Stravinsky into this impressive circle. Stravinsky was to become a close friend of both Debussy and Ravel, inspiring both men to further artistic experiments and encouraging them to take up fresh challenges. At his prompting, both Frenchmen began to study the works of Arnold Schoenberg and his Viennese circle, and readily agreed with Diaghilev to produce a ballet score on the theme of Daphnis and Chloe.

The ballet was premièred in 1912 after years of struggle with the score and bickering with the Ballets Russes and its director. The première was a disappointment, and the work was dropped. Happily, though, a revival soon after saw it claim its rightful place as one of this century's great ballet scores. Soon after this, Europe began the dark descent into the Great War of 1914–18.

The Great War

Like so many artists, Ravel found the war a horrific experience. He was shaken to the core not only by the terrible waste of lives but also by the sense of impending doom hanging over a culture he had done so much in the previous ten years to define. Being a man wholly caught up in questions of aesthetics, and who strove for 'balance and clarity in all things', Ravel's first reaction to the war was predictably non-partisan. He knew how much the strength of European culture relied on the cross-fertilization of ideas between nations and so refused to condemn all Germans and Austrians, as many were doing. At the same time he was aware how dear France was to him.

But what clearly gave him most heartache was the problem of leaving his mother at home while both he and his brother were at the front. Edouard had already volunteered and been accepted by September 1914, and Maurice, after agonies of indecision, volunteered a month later, only to be rejected as

death of his mother in 1917, while he was still recovering from dysentery. He was immediately discharged from the army, and after the funeral was thrown into deep despair. The years after the war found him at a low ebb, and he began to suffer from the insomnia which was to progressively worsen for the rest of his life. His private grief was expressed in the piano work, *Le Tombeau de Couperin,* while *La Valse* is a seeming valedictory glance at an irretrievable world.

Le Belvédère

From 1921 onwards he divided his life between the Paris home of his now-married brother, and a little house he bought, christened Le Belvédère, in a village called Montfort-l'Amaury, with a truly magnificent view over the Ile de France. The developing of this shell-like house into the eccentric and immaculate home it became, slowly helped pull Ravel out of his long depression.

Ravel decorated the house lovingly, designing and painting elaborate friezes in the rooms, and filling the house with finely crafted ornaments. He had a cultivated taste for the exotic, and Japanese prints and mechanical birds figure heavily in the perfect, polished rooms. Ravel's fascination with clockwork toys was legendary – so much so that Stravinsky was inclined to believe that they inspired his music. The composer of *The Rite of Spring* derided Ravel as 'a Swiss watchmaker'. But Ravel had a mischievious sense of humour, deliberately mixing real master-pieces with blatant imitations in his decorations, and his artifice in music may well have the same knowingness.

Ravel was immensely happy at Le Belvédère, but increasingly found himself isolated from the world. So many of his contemporaries had already gone, including Debussy, and a new generation of com-posers was emerging who looked not to him, but to Erik Satie once again. And, as a man who retained his

Ravel worked on the score for the ballet music of Daphnis and Chloé *(set design above) for about three years. When the ballet was first performed it had a disappointing reception but when revived shortly afterwards it received great acclaim.*

Like many of his contemporaries Ravel found the Great War of 1914–18 a shattering experience. He volunteered in 1914 but was rejected because he was underweight. In 1915, however, he was accepted in the army and was posted as a truck driver (above right) to the Verdun front.

underweight – he weighed just 98 pounds. By this time, however, his resolve had hardened, and he was tenacious in his efforts to be inducted. He was finally accepted in 1915, and was posted as a truck driver behind the Verdun front. He said on another occasion 'One must have a head and have guts, but never a heart.' Here, in a strange way, he had lived up to his words.

The war did not cost Ravel or his family as dear as it did most of his contemporaries. Both he and his brother survived intact, Maurice himself being invalided out in March 1917 with dysentery. He remained cheerful and communicative with his friends back in Paris, and was quick to comment publicly on the jingoistic and myopic thinking behind the establishment in 1916 of the National League for the Defence of French Music. He commented.

It would actually be damaging to French composers to ignore the output of their foreign colleagues ... Our art of music, at present so rich, would soon degenerate and restrict itself to obsolete academic formulas.

The greatest single tragedy of Ravel's war was the

From 1921 onwards Ravel divided his time between the Paris home of his brother Edouard and a house which he had bought in the village of Montfort-l'Amaury. His interest in the house (right), called Le Belvédère, helped pull him out of a long depression after the death of his mother in 1917.

In 1925 Ravel completed the music for a work in which he collaborated with the novelist Colette – L'enfant et les sortilèges, the title page of which is shown below. In the work, the magical world of childhood is re-created.

anti-establishment stance, even to the point of refusing to accept the Legion of Honour awarded him in 1920 – he claimed no one asked him first – he had no other natural social group to fall in with.

It is difficult to know entirely how Ravel felt at this time, for he remained all his life an intensely private, almost secretive, man, retaining the total reserve he claimed to have inherited from his mother. His sexual life, just as his compositional techniques, remain a complete mystery. There was some speculation that he was homosexual, but there is no evidence either way. While we cannot say that he had a physical liaison with either a man or a woman, we cannot say that he did not either.

Outwardly he remained a refined, extremely cultured, affable man – a man who derived tremendous pleasure and amusement from the best things in life. His lack of widespread acceptance never seemed to bother him at all. Ravel was quite happy entertaining his close friends with his legendary gourmet meals, as impeccable and original as his music, and smoking his beloved Caporal cigarettes.

The 'twenties'

The following decade was to see a number of important compositions flow from the composer's pen, such as the Violin Sonata, the Two Piano Concertos, and the opera *L'Enfant et les Sortilèges*. A

great many of these works were influenced by the jazz craze that swept through Europe in the 1920s. Ravel loved the spontaneous spirit of jazz and its expressiveness, and adopted its rhythms in many of his works.

Another important influence on Ravel was revealed in the opera, *L'Enfant et les Sortilèges* which was written in collaboration with the famous novelist Colette, who he had first met in 1900. In it Ravel basked in the world of childhood fantasy which it conjured up, giving it all his tenderness and love. For in a sense, Ravel never grew up, holding on tenaciously to every aspect of his own happy childhood as long as he could.

Still, there was a living to be made, and the premières of these works, plus the series of concert tours which he embarked upon in 1922 in London and continued every year up to 1926 in Europe, certainly helped Ravel to become more self-sufficient than at any other time in his life. He even played *La Valse* in Vienna, where he stayed as a guest of Mahler's widow Alma. Although she did not find his dandyism overwhelmingly attractive she appreciated his elegance. She recalled that 'he was a narcissist . . . who came to breakfast rouged and perfumed . . . and related all things to his bodily and facial charms. Though short, he was so well-proportioned, with such elegance and such elastic mobility of figure that he seemed quite beautiful.'

It was during the late 1920s that his music was first committed to disc with his own approval. His String Quartet was recorded in accordance with his own

composer continued to work on both his music and his concert commitments. The change in economical climate occasioned by the 1929 crash had very little effect on him, and he continued to live his refined existence. He was still capable of acts of great warmth towards his friends, however. When the pianist Paul Wittgenstein, who had lost his right hand in the war, approached him for a work, Ravel responded with the inspired and moving *Concerto for the Left Hand.*

This and its companion concerto from the same year, 1931, attest to the composer's artistic and personal well-being; and there seemed no reason to doubt that this state of affairs would continue indefinitely. Tragically, this was not to be the case.

A tragic accident

In October 1932 he was in a taxi which collided with another vehicle. He received head injuries which at

In 1928 Ravel (above) made a highly successful tour of the United States. During the visit he gave both private and public performances at venues ranging from Carnegie Hall to private homes (above right). Although he was thrilled by his reception and impressed by the generosity and hospitality of his hosts Ravel was glad to return to France. Over the next few years his artistic and personal well-being continued to grow. Sadly, however, after a motor accident in 1932 his health gradually declined and he died after an operation in 1937.

views, and he was quick to see the opportunities offered by the gramophone:

It will constitute a real document for posterity to consult . . . if only we had gramophone records approved by Chopin himself! Even with Debussy a great chance was lost.

The following year, 1928, saw his first tour of the United States of America. It went phenomenally well. Travelling with a wardrobe which included 50 silk shirts and 20 pairs of pyjamas, Ravel was fêted on both seaboards and thoroughly enjoyed all but two aspects of the trip. Being a committed gourmet, used to the best in French cooking, he was often affronted by food that was either second-rate or not highly seasoned enough. He was also increasingly at the mercy of crippling insomnia. And as the tour progressed, for it lasted five months, his health deteriorated rapidly. So, regardless of the huge financial and personal success of the tour, he was greatly relieved to reach France again.

The rest of the year proved to be just as profitable for him. His new orchestral piece, *Bolero,* proved wildly popular, and made him a household name. Ravel was pleased, but unemotional. He commented, 'I have written just one masterpiece, and that is the *Bolero.* Unfortunately, it is devoid of music.' However, he was pleased to accept an honorary degree in music from Oxford University, in recognition of his achievements.

In this period of increasing fame and security, the

the time seemed no more than slight concussion. But later, it became clear something was deeply amiss. He was unable to concentrate properly any more, and towards the end of the following year his bodily movements were no longer under the control of his brain. As the condition worsened, he lost proper control even over the power of speech. Saddest of all was the fact that he never wrote another composition after the accident.

What made this doubly tragic was that his brain continued to function perfectly inside his increasingly unreliable body. He was trapped inside his own infirmities, leaving him sometimes in impotent rages, at other times with a resigned equanimity.

In his last years Ravel stayed at his house at Montfort or with friends. He seemed happiest walking alone, or attending concerts. During this time his close and devoted friends did their utmost to help distract him from his suffering.

Finally, after a harrowing summer in 1937, it was decided that an operation should be risked. In December he was opened up and his brain examined. No irregularity was found. He regained consciousness, only to fall into a coma a few hours later from which he never recovered. He died on 28 December.

The cruellest blow perhaps was the fact that the man who had once said 'basically the only love affair I have ever had was with music' was unable to release the music he'd heard inside his head for the last five years of his life.

Orchestral works

From the mesmeric rhythm of Bolero – Ravel's *most popular orchestral piece – to the anarchy of* La Valse, *these five varied and vibrant dances show the composer at his colourful best.*

Bolero

One morning Ravel went to his piano and picked out a tune using just one finger. 'Don't you think', he asked a friend, 'this tune has an insistent quality about it? I shall try to repeat it a number of times without any development at all, increasing my orchestra as best I can'.

This seemingly trivial incident coincided with a request from the dancer, Ida Rubinstein, who asked Ravel for a ballet score based on orchestrations of pieces from Albeniz's *Iberia*. Soon after Ravel started work, however, it was discovered that the Spanish conductor, Enrique Arbos, held the copyright. On hearing of Ravel's interest in the piece, Arbos generously offered to renounce his rights, but Ravel was now piqued into doing a piece of his own, based on the simple melody line he had already discovered. The result, at first entitled *Fandango,* was written in five months and first performed at the Paris Opera on 22 November, 1928, as *Bolero.* The story is simple. A young woman begins to dance a languid bolero in a dimly lit café and, gradually, the other customers sit up and take notice. They become increasingly intoxicated by the bolero rhythm and the dance ends in a climax of ecstasy.

The première was a modest success that gave little indication of the sequence of events to come. Yet, in next to no time, as Ravel's biographer Roland-Manuel records,

When Ida Rubinstein (above), the leader of an outstanding ballet company and personal friend of Ravel's, asked him to compose a piece of music for her, he created the brilliant Bolero.

'large and small orchestras everywhere appropriated it . . . gramophone and radio repeated it all day long. The butcher boy whistled it and all the street answered him'. *Bolero* continues to reach people far beyond the usual audience for classical music, whether via the 1934 Paramount film or the 1984 World Ice Dance Championship. Ravel may have regretted that his name was universally known only as one half of the phrase 'Ravel's Bolero', but his sense of irony was acute enough to remark, on overhearing someone describe *Bolero* as 'madness', that this was 'the correct interpretation.'

Programme notes

Bolero consists of a single long tune, in two halves, repeated over and over during a long crescendo (17 minutes was Ravel's timing). The only variation is in volume and orchestral colour – even the accompanying rhythm and (until just before the end) the key are unchanging. It is an experiment in rising tension, using very limited means, but carried out with formidable control and, above all, orchestral mastery.

The three purely musical elements are presented at the outset: a stamping bass in plucked violas and cellos marking out the strong beats like a flamenco dancer's clapping; a rhythm on sidedrum designed to evoke rather than imitate the Spanish bolero dance of the 18th century; and, on solo flute in the fourth bar, one of the most famous tunes in Western music:

Example 1

Very softly, the clarinet now repeats this first half of the tune, while the flute takes up the sidedrum rhythm. The volume increases very slightly *(mezzo-piano)* as a high solo bassoon plays the second half of the tune. The shrill little E flat clarinet then repeats the second half of the tune and closes the first section. Each of the next three sections follows the same AABB pattern — first half of the tune, repeat, second half of the tune, repeat.

The second section opens on the oboe d'amore (an obsolete instrument which,

when he heard it, disappointed Ravel). The dynamic marking is still mezzo-piano, but the second violins now join the violas and cellos in pacing out the bass tread. For the repeat, Ravel has the horns quite high up, adding their colour to the sidedrum rhythm, while the melody is given to flute and muted trumpet. For the second half of the tune, the trumpet has the sidedrum rhythm and we now hear one of the most characteristic timbres of *Bolero* – the tenor saxophone, whose jazz associations are a reminder of how much Ravel loved to sit in Parisian cafés, smoking and talking for as long as the band would play! The repeat is given almost entirely to the high-pitched

sopranino saxophone except for the last few bars where the low pitch of the melody require the soprano saxophone to take over.

The third section opens with an example of Ravel's superb imagination; celesta, horn and piccolos – the most unlikely combination in the whole score – play the theme in three different keys. The aim is clarity, not blend, not dissonance but a magical 'chiming'. This chiming quality carries into the repeat, where a conventional wind band is used. The Moorish quality of the second half of the theme now sounds wild and exotic as the volume rises to *mezzo-forte* (moderately

loud) and a solo trombone glides *(glissando)* into action. Flutes, violas and a horn insist on the sidedrum rhythm, as a fuller version of the chiming wind instruments completes the section.

In the next part, the strings are finally given the melody, first as a single line, then enriching the repeat by playing in chords. The second half is introduced by a far heavier stamping of the bass by winds, trombones and tuba. The orchestration gets even fuller as the tension mounts: the trumpet adds its voice to the second half melody, while the trombones and lower strings join the repeat.

What can Ravel think of next? He embarks

First performed as part of a short ballet which takes part in a dimly lit café scene in Barcelona (above), Bolero *entranced thousands with its brilliant orchestral shading and a curiously hypnotic quality derived from the tempo.*

on a *fifth* section, as winds chant the sidedrum rhythm and the scream of the trumpet dominates the tune. But, instead of the expected repeat, we swing straight into the second half, raising the excitement even higher as Ravel uses his final *coup de théâtre.* After 300 bars of the same key, the whole orchestra suddenly shifts. The effect is to raise the hysteria to fever pitch; the trombones roar their abandon,

MAURICE RAVEL

9.1226
8

MIROIRS

POUR PIANO

I. Noctuelles
II. Oiseaux tristes
III. Une barque sur l'Océan
IV. Alborada del gracioso
V. La vallée des cloches

En recueil, prix net : 10 fr.

Paris, E. DEMETS, Éditeur

Originally part of a set of piano pieces, **Miroirs** *(above),* **Alborada** del gracioso *was transcribed into a superb work for full orchestra.*

the music crashes back to the previous key, staggering to its orgiastic final fling and, with a last cry of despair, or delight, *Bolero* collapses.

Miroirs: Alborada del gracioso

In 1905 Ravel wrote a set of piano pieces called *Miroirs* (Mirrors), a title drawn from the pictorial and evocative mood of some of the pieces. Ravel subsequently transcribed two of them for orchestra, *Une barque sur l'ocean* and *Alborada del gracioso*. Alborada means 'morning song' and gracioso was the sharp-witted 'fool' of Spanish classical plays. The literal translation of 'joker's dawn song' is so clumsy it seems best left in Spanish!

The Alborada began Ravel's brief period of obsession with Spanish topics such as the *Rapsodie espagnole*. Unlike the evening mood of the Rapsodie, however, this is a morning piece where the sultry night has given way to a fierce Mediterranean glare.

Programme notes

The work is launched with a vibrant Iberian dance rhythm, vigorously plucked by strings. Flashing harp scales lead to an attractively lighthearted oboe tune and the subsequent 'strumming' effects in the strings evoke a flamenco guitar. The sudden loud passage exults to the first phrase of the oboe tune, with strings, trumpets and tambourine prominent. A repeated-note figure appears first in the

The portrait of an Infanta (right), by the great 17th-century artist Velázquez, encapsulates the stately elegance and somewhat melancholy mood of Ravel's evocative Pavane pour une Infante défunte.

trumpets and then the horns, separated by skirling woodwind runs. The opening rhythm reappears in the gossamer texture of harp, strings and flute, and the music comes to a sudden stop on a short but loud chord.

The middle section begins with a high, poignant solo for bassoon, twice interrupted by a rhythmic passage for glittering percussion. The strings respond to the bassoon by lamenting with a dark, Hispanic passion. Then they rear up in protest, punctuated by loud interjections from the full orchestra and return to their smouldering theme despite another attempt to lift them out of their sultry brooding. These dark thoughts are banished by the reappearance of the opening rhythm as the final section begins.

All the themes of the first section are now paraded in turn but this time, undeterred by the solo violin reminiscing on the middle section or by other relapses into slow music, they are driven on into one of the most exciting finales in orchestral music. The themes tumble over each other with hectic energy until, at the very end, the trombones call out 'enough'.

Pavane pour une Infante Défunte

Ravel's intention was to evoke a vision of the Spanish court at the time of the Renaissance, hence the *Infante,* or Spanish princess. The title (Pavane for a dead Infante) was invented simply because Ravel liked the sound of the words and not because of any hidden meaning, but the composer became exasperated with the

piece and the literal interpretation of it. The sentimental way it was played led him to protest that it was the princess that was dead, not the pavane!

Programme notes

Although marked slow, the walking bass we hear at the start makes it clear that this is a dance, however stately, while the plucked strings suggest the 16th-century lutenist accompanying the dancers. The melody, one of Ravel's most immediately pleasing, is played by horns with echoes from other woodwind at the ends of phrases. A characteristic of this pavane is the broad gesture placed at the end of each section. The solo oboe plays a new but similar theme, accompanied by the other

By permission of the British Library

The simple construction of the piano version of Ravel's **Pavane** *(above), its salon charm and sad title all helped to boost its popularity.*

winds and the harp. The strings repeat this and the opening theme returns on the woodwinds. The third theme is now heard high on the oboe, but again is of such similar cast to the others as to sustain a feeling of tenderness for bygone days. This is repeated, lead by the flute and indispensable Ravelian brushstrokes of harp colour. The opening tune comes round for the last time, played by strings over the harp's lute imitation, and this broad gesture rounds off the work.

Rapsodie espagnole

This, the Spanish Rhapsody, was written in 1907, though one of the movements, the *Habañera* was written in 1897, as part of a piano work called *Sites auriculaires.* Debussy admired it so much that he asked to borrow the score and Ravel was understandably annoyed when Debussy's *Soirées dans Grenade* appeared in 1903 and featured its habanera rhythm!

Understanding music: Ravel's contemporaries

During the last years of the 19th century and the early years of the 20th, music in Ravel's France was the product of an uneasy co-existence of an older, romantic school deriving from Wagner which centred on the pupils of César Franck (1822–90), and a newer one related to contemporary trends in Impressionist painting and Symbolist literature, which focussed on Debussy. With the outbreak of war in 1914, both these schools fell into disfavour with Ravel's generation. There was a natural reaction against Germany – and that included music based on German models – and also against some of Debussy's imitators.

The new movement, founded in a spirit of rebellion, relied much on the music and personality of Erik Satie (1866–1925). Although a musician of the older generation who had influenced both Ravel and Debussy, Satie had never, like them, become a central figure in French music. His works, deceptively simple and unassuming, often bore bizarre titles such as 'Three pieces in the shape of a pear', and exhibited a cool, mocking character that mirrored his own personal reputation for sardonic wit and eccentricity. His ballet score, *Parade,* for example, includes the use of a revolver, a siren and a typewriter, and was written for Diaghilev in collaboration with Picasso and Jean Cocteau.

Cocteau's book, *Le coq et l'arlequin,* was the manifesto for the new age, deriding German compositions as 'music to be listened to with the head in the hands', praising Satie and recommending the new American jazz for its direct, primitive virtues. Paris in the 1920s was once again the centre of artistic fashion. Great works were produced nevertheless, for this was still the Paris of Stravinsky and Diaghilev, of Proust and Joyce. But the spirit of the age was one of wit and elegance – a spirit supposedly embodied by 'Les Six'.

'Les Six' was the group of French composers referred to by Henri Collet – *'Les cinqs russes, les six français, et M. Satie'* (the five Russians, the six French and M. Satie). Not that Francis Poulenc (1899-1963), Louis Durey (1888-1979), Georges Auric (1899-1983), Germaine Tailleferre (1892-1983), Darius Milhaud (1892-1974) and Arthur Honegger (1892-1955) were a close-knit group. Durey moved away from the group to become a socialist; the graceful, feminine music of Germaine Tailleferre, the one woman member of the group, was soon eclipsed by the more astringent compositions of

Milhaud and Poulenc; Honegger's Swiss background made him more sympathetic to the German tradition as his five symphonies show, and he had never much time for Satie; while Auric remained a collaborator with Cocteau in his later film career.

But it was Milhaud and Poulenc who most kept faith with the ideals of *Le coq et l'arlequin.* Milhaud was particularly adept at incorporating jazz idioms in his works. His ballet, *La Creation du monde* (1923) uses a saxophone and much percussion in an explicitly 'bluesy' idiom. Another feature of Milhaud's style is its harmonic spice, frequently deriving from his fondness for combining two different keys. Poulenc also employed jazz in some of his works but his style has more *tendresse.* Poulenc's most successful work of the period, *Les Biches* (1924) contains an exquisite and affecting Adagietto, full of a melancholy beauty.

It would be easy to assume that French music at this time meant the music of Paris, were it not for the work of Albert Roussel (1869–1937). Roussel, who came to music rather late in life, lived on the Normandy coast from 1921 onwards. He was influenced by music he had heard on his honeymoon in India, and this gives an exotic flavour to such works as the orchestral *Evocations* (1915) and to his opera, *Padmâvatî* (1918). His best known piece is his ballet score, *Bacchus et Ariane* (1930) which has an exhilarating rhythmic drive, testifying to the continuing influence of Stravinsky upon French composers. It also has a certain intellectual rigour and an absence of the frivolity of some of his musical compatriots. But French music would be poorer without the confections filled with Parisian charm and wit, such as *L'horloge de Flore* of Jean Francaix (b. 1912), which is full of neo-classical allusions; or the *Divertissement* of Jacques Ibert (1890–1962), written as incidental music to the play, and *The Italian Straw Hat,* full of mock references to Viennese waltzes and Mendelssohn.

France continued to produce new artistic schools, whether training establishments, such as the American Conservatory from which Nadia Boulanger taught a whole generation of American composers, or groups of individuals such as *La Jeune France,* founded in 1936 and boasting Olivier Messiaen as its most important member, who, along with his pupil Pierre Boulez, upholds the finest traditions of French music.

Ravel's Rapsodie espagnole *(above) was one of a long and distinguished line of musical works inspired by romantic Spanish themes.*

Programme notes

Although Ravel did not know Spain personally, he was able to represent the moods and colours of the country, as de Falla said, 'by a free use of the modal rhythms and melodies and ornamental figures of Spanish popular music, none of which has altered in any way the natural style of the composer'. The *Rapsodie* is in four movements.

1 Prélude à la Nuit: très modéré

The entire movement of *Prelude to the Night* is built on a falling four-note phrase, F, E, D, C sharp, heard very quietly right at the start and for much of the movement. It sets up at once the hypnotic mood of warm, languid Southern nights. An occasional sigh from the winds and shimmering string phrases barely interrupt the stillness of the atmosphere. Then, with a wash of harp tone, the strings stir themselves into a passionate phrase which soars briefly only to fall back again in a mood of heady sensuality. There is a florid clarinet cadenza and the four-note motif, oppressive as the airless night, returns on the tinkling tones of the celesta. The bassoon has the cadenza, the strings have the four-note motif and the celesta has the last word.

2 Malaguena: assez vif

The piece begins with a shadowy but very rhythmic introduction before the main theme is given by the trumpet and a *tambour de basque* (tambourine).

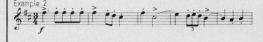

The violins take up the theme, but trumpets quickly reclaim it, provoking a surge from the full orchestra. A solo cor anglais rhapsodizes in a series of Moorish-sounding arabesques over vaporous harp glissandi, returning to the mood of the Prelude and leading to a momentary return of its four-note motif. The wispy, muted rhythms of the opening are heard once more and the *malaguena* simply evaporates.

3 Habañera: assez lent et d'un rhythme las

A languid, seductive quality pervades this piece, marked 'slow and with a weary rhythm'. In atmosphere another nocturnal piece, its haunting quality derives partly from the persistent C sharp pedal (continuously sustained note) first on clarinets, then ingeniously given to each department of the orchestra in turn. The horns play the habañera rhythm and woodwind carry the main tune, which is developed in the sweet tones of two violins and viola and expires in the sighing of horns. Although all the violins now beckon us and the rhythm is more pronounced, an air of infinite lassitude prevails and the *Habañera,* like the two previous movements, dies away.

4 Feria: assez animé

The *Feria* (festival) is by far the liveliest of the four movements. It perhaps owes a debt to Chabrier, whom Ravel greatly admired:

certainly it has the same festive, even raucous quality of his *Espana.* Again, the piece opens quietly. Harps and piccolos, an ethereal combination, announce a feathery, rhythmic oscillation. This leads to repeated-note fanfares associated with orchestral *espagnolerie* and builds to a crashing tutti with much use of percussion and heavy brass. A carefree dance ture breaks the mood, becoming especially spirited when heard in the braying of the french horns:

Example 3

Again the activity increases, the volume swells and the crashing tutti recurs, this time going over the top and collapsing as the carnival crowd disperses. Suddenly, a drunken double-bass meanders across the scene (the violin sighs must be the nearest thing in music to a hangover). A sympathetic cor anglais comforts him with another languorous theme. The mood and the four-note motif of the Prelude return. But so, before long, do the revellers – heralded by surges in the strings singing their now familiar songs. This time the climax is even more exuberant, so wild as to risk spoiling the good nature of the piece. There is the briefest respite to this orchestral riot, before the final whirlwind

As if drugged by the warm night air, sleepy Spaniards doze outside a tavern (left). The orchestra too, seems seduced by the soporific charm of the music as it ripples through Prélude à la Nuit – the opening movement in Ravel's Rapsodie espagnole.

brings *Rapsodie espagnole* to a boisterous close.

La Valse

As early as 1906, Ravel had toyed with the idea of a symphonic poem to be called *Wien* (Vienna), as a sort of homage to Johann Strauss. The project languished until Diaghilev asked Ravel to complete a piece for the 1920 season of the Ballets Russes. This lifted him out of his creative impasse and, in 1919, he happily wrote '… I'm waltzing madly'. By early 1920, Ravel was ready to play the score to Diaghilev.

He and Marcelle Meyer played the two-piano version and quite soon Diaghilev's discomfort became evident. When they finished, he said 'Ravel it is a masterpiece, but it is not a ballet … It is the portrait of a ballet'. Ravel said nothing, but quietly took his score and left the room.

Programme notes

La Valse, as Ravel renamed the work, was first performed as a concert piece in December 1920 and not staged as a ballet until 1928, a long time for him to have to

Gonzalo Bilbao 'Summer Night in Seville'. Museo Provincial de Bellas Artes, Seville/AISA

Awash with colour and boisterous enthusiasm, the friendly chaos of a Spanish festival (right) sweeps through Feria, *the last and longest (it occupies 50 of the score's 89 pages) of the four movements in* Rapsodie espagnole.

Sorolla 'Sevilla. The Dance'. Hispanic Society of America

" LA VALSE "

Mauro Pucciarelli-Roma

A set design for La Valse *(above), the work which Ravel intended as a ballet and confidently described as a 'choreographic poem'.*

wait. He seems all along to have had a sketchy scenario in mind and wrote:

Through whirling clouds, waltzing couples may be faintly distinguished. The clouds gradually scatter; one sees . . . an immense hall peopled with a whirling crowd. The scene is gradually

In response to a request from the dynamic Russian impresario Diaghilev (below), Ravel composed La Valse *for the Ballets Russes.*

BBC Hulton Picture Library

illuminated. The light of the chandeliers bursts forth at fortissimo . . . An Imperial court, about 1855.

This seems to invite staging but, on listening to *La Valse* it is easy to see why Diaghilev was concerned. The waltzes emerge from a mist, only to be lost again or become frenetic, even hostile – and at the end a violence reminiscent of Stravinsky's *Rite of Spring* actually destroys them.

Ravel, who described the work as a choreographic poem, later recalled that he

intended a sort of apotheosis of the waltz, 'linked, in my mind, with a kind of fatal and fantastic whirling.'

The work begins with a low rumble and snatches of waltz tunes groping through on bassoons. The mood brightens as strings and high woodwind hint at more of a melody, until at last the strings play the whole theme, its suavity underlined by the downward swoops:

Example 4

Harps rush up and down, the theme really begins to waltz, the dance becomes heady and the volume increases, the brass adds its weight to the final emphatic cadence and a new waltz immediately begins, first on wind instruments then on strings. Again, a fortissimo passage for trumpets and trombones announces the next dance, its themes again developed by strings but this time the outcome is a repeated insistence on a loud three-note phrase thumped out by the brass and bass drum (divided by swirling wind phrases). A new waltz breaks through in strings, a loud climax peaks out and a languorous 'after the ball' mood pervades. The murky opening material returns and again the three-note phrase is given to heavy brass, this time with the repetitions rising breathlessly upward and followed by a hectic, nightmarish succession of distorted tunes. The final onset of chaos is announced by a bold striding tune blasted out on trombones. Then, apart from one deeply affecting two-bar appeal from the strings for sanity to return, the forces of destruction annihilate all the charm and sophistication that the waltz ever stood for.

FURTHER LISTENING

Gaspard de la Nuit
Ravel was, first and foremost, a composer who wrote at the piano and for the piano. Most of his greatest orchestral pieces started life as piano works. *Gaspard,* the supreme pinnacle of his pianistic writings, was never orchestrated – and little wonder, for there are many passages of stupendous technical difficulty, especially in the third and last movement, *Scarbo.* Throughout Ravel exhibits his wonderful understanding of the piano's sonorities to produce chilling moods such as in *Le Gibet,* or the impression of liquid grace and charm which is so central to the opening movement, *Ondine.*

Introduction and Allegro
During his lifetime, Ravel wrote many fine chamber works, some purely instrumental, and some employing the human voice. This work for harp, clarinets, flute and string quartet is one of the most refined creations of a man noted for his refinement. The choice of instruments clearly aids the

general translucency of the ensemble textures, but the writing itself is remarkable for its gentle grace and elegance. Every bar of the work testifies to Ravel's sensuality.

L'Enfant et les Sortilèges
All his life Ravel was fascinated and inspired by childhood in all its different incarnations. Thus this operatic collaboration with the novelist Colette, which deals with a naughty child being gently upbraided and taught a valuable lesson by his own toys and pets, is a work which at each turn benefits from the loving care Ravel lavished upon it. Ravel's ingenious treatment of the animals and inanimate objects that come to life is bewitchingly magical, yet he also captures the potential malevolence of an ordinary room as seen by a child. The work is certainly not part of the grand opera tradition: the scale must be intimate, the characters childlike. It is a fantasy world which must retain its innocence, and this Ravel was wholly successful in achieving.

'Universal nationalism'

After years of political upheaval, 19th-century France entered a period of rich artistic expression inspired by the passionate individuality of her impoverished neighbour – Spain.

Throughout the 19th century, Spain stood out as the poor and battle-weary cousin of the European family. Unlike her wealthy neighbours (particularly Britain and France), she was almost totally without any kind of 'middle class' to provide a buffer between the extremes in her society. Political issues were decided by three main interest groups: landowners, clergy and the military, but resentment was growing. The spent wealth of many lesser nobles led to discontent and jealous rivalries among their ranks and, at the bottom of the scale, the peasants were involved in frequent uprisings and outbreaks of civil disorder.

Together these factors provided the ingredients for a total collapse of the social order and, on top of everything else, the country was wracked by bitter disputes over the legitimate succession to the throne. Having no sons, the ruling king, Ferdinand VII, 'changed the rules' so that his infant daughter (Isabella) could succeed him. After his death in 1833, the three-year-old princess was duly proclaimed queen, with her mother as regent. But the new edict was bitterly resented and rival factions clashed head on – opposition to the queen being spearheaded by supporters of her uncle, Don Carlos. Clinging to power, Isabella remained queen until 1868, when her blighted rule was ended by violent revolution. Continued disputes over the vacant throne embroiled not only Spain, but the external interests of France and Britain as well. In an effort to

The wild, free spirit of Spain – a country of rugged beauty, dazzling sunshine and earthy passions – enthralled the 19th-century French Romantics and became a major source of artistic inspiration.

Nineteenth-century Spain was a country of many contrasts. The gulf between the wealthy, opulent upper classes (above) – dominated to a large extent by the clergy – and the poverty-stricken peasants (right) fuelled the fires of discontent and civil disorder.

fill the vacuum, the Spanish crown was at first offered to an Italian prince (Amadeo), but his moderate rule ended in an abrupt abdication. The brief spell of republicanism which followed soon gave way to the royalists – this time led by the supporters of Isabella's son Alfonso – and the monarchy was once more restored.

Such endemic civil war, coupled with continuous interference from outside (and mostly Anglo-French) interests contrived to make Spain one of the unhappiest countries in Europe; as her neighbours grew in power and wealth, the contrast with her poverty and instability was made even sharper. In general, the population of Europe had almost doubled over the preceding century, thanks to improvements in areas like agriculture, science and medicine and, in Britain, the heralds of the industrial revolution, even greater prosperity and urbanization pointed the way to the future. But in more isolated areas such as Spain, these developments made little impact – her agriculture continued to be backward and her industry was almost non-existent.

Universal nationalism

Despite her wealth, France too suffered from political upheaval through much of the 19th century. The radical republicanism that led to Louis-Philippe's downfall in 1848, also led, within three years, to the coup d'état by Louis Napoleon (Emperor Napoleon III). After defeat by the Germans in 1870, the emperor in turn was replaced by the anarchic Paris Commune, before relative stability was at last achieved by the Third Republic. During its short period of success, the Second Empire was, never-theless, a time of brilliant artistic achievements and considerable opulence, especially in Paris. The 1850s and 1860s saw a rich profusion of art and music, while the contrasting styles of different but outstanding generations overlapped to produce interest, controversy and inspiration.

Many Frenchmen were still deeply imbued with Revolutionary ideals of individualism, anticlericalism and, above all, the right to freedom of expression and thought. Under this impetus, and in an inevitable reaction to the 19th century obsession with 'scientific method', a new surge of Romanticism was born. The mood was later summed up by the French artist Renoir:

Nowadays they want to explain everything. But if they could explain a picture it wouldn't be art. Shall I tell you what I think are the two qualities of art? It must be indescribable and it must be inimitable . . . A work or art must seize hold of you, enfold you, carry you away. It is the means by which the artist conveys his passion; it is a current which he transmits and which sweeps you up in his passion.

The idealists recognized no frontiers to expression, no limit to artistic treatment and, by experimenting freely with all or any inspiration, they sought new ideas from around the world – so coining the phrase 'universal nationalism' (a nationalism, for example, based on Spanish folk music but developing it within the sophisticated techniques of the French or Italian tradition).

One result of this was the artistic exploration of a formerly ignored source – the people. Their every-day lives, their struggle for survival and the earthy passions in their lives brought to light a world unfettered by the artificial value of the bourgeois

élite. The French also proved susceptible to another source – the new international contacts of the post-Napoleonic period. They eagerly absorbed influences from Germany, the Orient, Japan, the Arab world and Russia, but most of all they looked to Spain. Here, the arts had never been straitjacketed by minority tastes and, for example, would have rejected outright the rigid rules of an institute like the French Academy.

The lure of the South

The rugged, romantic appeal of her people and their seemingly indomitable spirit provided enchantment and allure: here was a land where the arts sprang directly from the soil, where the people had a fiery, pugnacious character and compulsive individualism. More than any other European country, it seemed that the history of Spain was the history of individuals, from the legendary conquistadores who had created the 16th-century Spanish empire to the local militias and rebel bands who had put up fierce and heroic resistance to the French in the Peninsular War of 1808–1814.

Spain, too, was unique in its rich tradition of folk music, songs and dances and in the tenacity with which she guarded this inheritance. The tradition was due in part to a long-established cycle of seasonal festivities associated with peasant life (and

Because of its enormous regional diversity, Spain boasted a uniquely rich tradition of folk music, song and dance. The colour and vibrancy of the flamenco fiesta (above) was just one of the many elements of peasant life that captured the imagination of Spain's more sedate neighbours.

little disrupted by the 'modernization' that was affecting other European countries) and partly to geography. To this day, the Iberian peninsula has a wealth of regional diversity thanks to the mountain chains which divide it and which provide remarkably effective cultural barriers. Like all countries, Spain has also experienced influences from various historic migration and invasions; in the 16th century, for example, the first gypsies crossed her borders, bringing with them the explosive vibrancy of Flamenco. In later years, fresh impetus resulted from her cultural ties with South America and her close proximity to France.

Proximity too, played its part in drawing the French south. There was a blurring of the frontier across the Pyrenees, where Basque and Catalan country spilled over into southern France and where local impulses were readily transmitted from one side to the other. As early as the 15th century, French literature had been directly influenced by Spanish

Whether in the sober portraits of the aristocracy (below) or in his gruesome emotive works depicting both real and imaginary horrors, Goya's works had a tremendous impact in France.

Goya 'La Marquise de la Solana'. Louvre, Paris/Réunion des musées nationaux

romances and folk stories and these ingredients reappeared in the 17th-century works of Corneille and Molière. In the 19th century, an upsurge of interest led to the classic Spanish story of Don Quixote being translated into French and it, in turn, provided rich material for many French composers. The Spanish 'romanceros' – folk poems of Spanish history and legend – were freely tapped by French writers and dramatists: Victor Hugo, Prosper Mérimée and Emile Deschamps were just some of the luminaries who used them as sources, thus injecting a fresh though savage vigour into French literature.

Even the world of the visual arts had little immunity to the infectious charm of these influences. An early but profound impact was made by the works of Francisco Goya y Lucientes (1746–1828). Goya had led a curious double life, producing orthodox portraits for members of the Spanish court on one hand, yet also creating deeply charged canvasses to highlight the piteous waste and cruelty of war and the gruesome fantasies from a black world of witches and warlocks.

The brutality and terror in Goya's work, its technical boldness, the rough, hasty texture and strong use of colour, gave a new, if uncomfortable jolt to the art world and deeply impressed French artists such as Eugène Delacroix (1798–1863) and, in later years, Edouard Manet (1832–1883).

Tourist Spain

Manet, the innovator and leader of the so-called Impressionist movement in art, was an ardent devotee of the Spanish master and was also deeply influenced by the 17th-century Spaniard, Velázquez. He was even accused of imitating directly their 'brilliant light effects and garish colours'.

Until 1865, however, Manet had never been to Spain: his was a culture acquired second-hand and, conveniently, out of context. Many of the subjects he painted were based on the colourful and picturesque troupe of Spanish dancers who visited Paris in 1862 and more than ever excited his enthusiasm for the 'tourist' Spain they represented. His whole attitude and approach was dramatically altered when he finally visited the country and was confronted by the harsh reality behind the glamorous façade so popular in Paris. After his return, Manet painted three bullfight scenes, but his Spanish phase was almost at an end – the poverty, dirt, illiteracy and preoccupation with death that he had encountered made far less attractive subjects than popular imaginings!

Bullfights, too, provided unexpected inspiration for one of France's great musicians, Debussy. Like Manet, Debussy only knew Spain from reading translations of great works, from pictures in the Paris galleries or from songs and dances performed by visiting troupes. At the Paris Exhibition of 1889/1890, he wandered about, listening intently to the extraordinary musical sounds gathered from around the world. But for him, Spanish music, especially from Andalusia, was outstanding. Curiously, he only crossed the borders into Spain on one occasion – to watch a bullfight in the frontier town of San Sebastian – yet he remembered the experience all his life. He vividly described the contrasting patterns of light falling across the ring, with one half in bright sunshine, the other deep in shade. These mixtures of light and shade, together with the drama of the fight itself, were transported into his music to create a powerful but purely imaginary evocation of Spain. Debussy, like Manet and so many other writers and musicians of his day, was not so much attempting to write 'Spanish' music, or create 'Spanish' paintings, rather he was translating into his own idiom the powerful associations that traditional images of Spain had aroused in him.

The triumph of Romance

While art and music were experimenting with new ideas and techniques, French literature and drama were also ready to explore fresh ground and many French writers looked across the Franco-Spanish borders for new ideas and romantic story lines. Victor Hugo (1802–1885) was a master of many forms; poetry, novels and drama. In the latter form, his aim was to conjure up Olympian visions of Man and History and his immediate model was

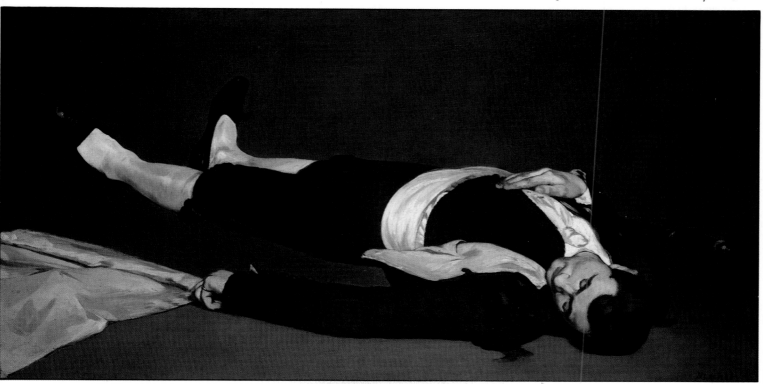

Cham's caricature **Incident in the Bull Ring** *(right) appeared in a French satirical magazine in 1864. It shows us what Manet's painting of the same name may have looked like (one of the two remaining portions of the work is the poignant* **Dead Toreador** *(below), but obviously the cartoonist did not share the painter's romantic view of Spain.*

Shakespeare. But, for his source material, Hugo turned to the Spanish romanceros and it was here that he found a basis for this melodramatic and highly controversial verse-play, *Hernani*.

Hernani was Hugo's assault on the decayed neoclassicism of the 18th-century French theatre. This antiquated convention had perpetuated the image but not the substance of the elegance and refinement achieved by the likes of Corneille, Molière and Racine. Their golden age had long passed, but the strict, formal rules of classical tragedy were still applied so rigidly that they debased character, action and credibility and, above all, had no relevance to human conditions. By the late 1820s, further barriers had been thrown up by restraints on the freedom of the press and by the severe censorship imposed by King Charles X. One of Hugo's plays (*Marion de Lorme*) had already fallen foul of the official censors and, for his riposte, Hugo presented French theatre-goers with a new and sensational drama – *Hernani*.

In the play, the hero is a disgraced nobleman, Hernani, whose lover is also courted by both the King of Spain and a powerful grandee (Don Gomez). The king unsportingly abducts the unfortunate señorita, leaving the hero to plan her rescue through an unlikely alliance with his remaining rival, Don Gomez. The price of the rescue is high, however, and Hernani has to promise that he will kill himself at the moment when Don Gomez sounds a golden horn. The young lovers are duly married but, on their wedding night, Don Gomez sounds the signal for suicide. The distraught bride faithfully shares her husband's cup of poison and Don Gomez, overcome with remorse, throws himself onto his sword.

The drama (which Giuseppe Verdi converted into his first successful opera, *Ernani* in 1844) was marked by high passion, fiery poetry and, for the ill-fated lovers, passages of great elegaic beauty. All this strength and heat so shocked the adherents of classicism that the first two performances – at the Comedie Française theatre in February 1830 –

Manet 'The Dead Toreador'. National Gallery of Art, Washington, Widener Collection 1942

resulted in violent clashes with Hugo's student supporters. The students were led by two flamboyant poets, Petrus Borel and Théophile Gautier (whose cherry-coloured doublet caused almost as much sensation as the play itself!). This rowdy band outclapped, outcheered and generally outmatched the staid supporters of classicism, won the day resoundingly for Hugo and helped to bring about a complete break with the past in terms of theatrical presentation.

Hugo's 'Cénacle' (literary circle) included a less volatile genius, Prosper Mérimée (1803-1870), one of France's greatest short story writers and a noted Hispanophile. Mérimée's strength in short fiction lay in his powerful delineation of characters and of situations in which they were driven to extremes by the strength of their own emotions. Spain, with its highly strung sense of personal honour, its underlying violence and Moorish fatalism, seemed tailormade for him. In addition to fiction, he wrote the scholarly *History of Spain* and a stylish biography of King Pedro I, (a 14th-century king of Castille) which is still considered a masterpiece. Like Hugo, Mérimée was drawn by the Spanish romanceros and these were the source of his series of plays, *Théâtre de Clara Azul* (1825) and his most celebrated story, *Carmen* (1845). Thirty years later, Georges Bizet took this story of gypsy sensuality, love, revenge and murder and the work he created from it did as much for opera as Hugo's *Hernani* had done for the theatre.

Despite the emotional force of Bizet's music, the libretto was a somewhat sanitized version of the Mérimée original. Mérimée's Carmen was a sluttish, unwashed gypsy, her husband was a deep-dyed villain and the Basque, Don José, far from being a lovelorn victim driven to desperation by Carmen's infidelity, was a thoroughgoing and murderous rascal in his own right.

On its publication in 1845, the novel was received by a reading public well versed in the dramatic realities of Romanticism; the reaction to the opera was far less sophisticated. Even before the first performance, Bizet's work was pilloried as obscene, immoral and unplayable, and the first choice for the title role refused the part because Bizet would not tone down the 'very scabrous side' of his heroine. The ultimate Carmen (Galli-Marie) performed the role with all the brazen sensuality required, only to be abused by critics who thought her interpretation deserving of police prosecution! Theatre goers and critics alike were stupefied by the scenes of unbridled passions now unveiled on the stage of the Opera Comique.

Honouring a debt

Even before he wrote Carmen, Bizet had been moving towards the Spanish idiom with his operas, but none of his music was 'Spanish' in a sense that any Spaniard would recognize. Carmen may be an opera about Spain, but it is a French opera nevertheless. Still decidedly French, but nearer the Spanish spirit, were the works of Maurice Ravel and Claude Debussy. Both composers had a natural empathy for the traditional folk music of regions like Andalusia and the idiosyncratic tones of their songs and dances. Debussy, in fact, interpreted more faithfully than any of his compatriots, the essence of flamenco – that vibrant mix of French café singer and Moorish rhythm, colourful costumes, violent movement and whirring castanets (which, like guitars, were Moorish instruments).

LES ROMAINS ÉCHEVELÉS A LA 1re REPRÉSENTATION D'HERNANI.

Hugo's sensational drama, Hernani, *based on Spanish romanceros, shocked French theatre goers by breaking every rule in the 'classical tragedy' book. Reaction was so strong that riots broke out during the first two performances (left).*

The drama of Spain and its colourful spectacles such as the bullfight (below) inspired the works of French musicians, particularly Ravel and Debussy.

The writer and noted Hispanophile, Prosper Mérimée brought to life the most famous gypsy of them all – Carmen (above). His story of passion and death later provided Bizet with the sensual heroine of his famous opera.

It was through the work of Claude Debussy that Spanish composers such as Isaac Albeniz and Mañuel de Falla were to become fully aware of the power and true worth of their own native music. De Falla (the frontispiece of his El Amor Brujo is shown on the right) is quoted as saying '. . . if Debussy used Spanish folk music to inspire some of his greatest works he has generously repaid us and it is now Spain which is indebted to him'.

Events finally seemed to come full cycle, when Debussy was praised by one of Spain's outstanding composers. Mañuel de Falla, who openly admired the authenticity and power of the Frenchman's music. Debussy had communicated his 'impressionistic' music to the young de Falla, influencing his work and advising him not to neglect the invaluable musical heritage of his native Andalucia. In 1920, two years after Debussy's death, de Falla acknowledged his obligation to and regard for the composer by writing a *Homage* to him, a piece of guitar music with echoes of Debussy's *Iberia.*

Debussy, Dukas, Vincent d'Indy, Camille Saint-Saens, Jules Massenet and other French composers were, in fact, remarkably hospitable to their Spanish counterparts – most notably Granados, Albeniz and de Falla – not simply as teachers or mentors but as performers championing their music and lifting their careers. Most vital were the practical returns that the Spaniards enjoyed from facilities which barely existed in Spain. At home there was no established musical infrastructure, no great opera house, no permanent orchestra of any size, no profusion of strong ensembles, no network of concert halls and no influential entrepreneurs. All these and more were made available in France and many personal as well as professional friendships flowered as a result of the exchange.

Manuel de Falla readily acknowledged his debt and regarded Paris as his second home; the seven years he spent in France (from 1907–1914) were crucial to his career. Without France and its opportunities, de Falla later said, he could have achieved nothing. He even went so far as to suggest that Debussy was not just a benevolent mentor and friend, but the virtual creator of modern Spanish music technique. To an extent this is true, though it took the talents of de Falla and Albeniz to wed 'impressionism' to the peculiar flavour of their native music before a truly distinctive Spanish mood emerged.

A new protégé

Towards the end of the century, the close contacts between France and Spain were about to produce yet another outstanding protégé; In 1896, a 16-year old Spaniard called Pablo Picasso wrote to a friend:

If I had a son who wanted to paint, I wouldn't let him live in Spain. And I don't think I would send him to Paris (where I would love to be myself), but to Munik (I don't know if it is spelt that way). It is a town where painting is studied seriously, without paying attention to such fashions as pointillism, which I am not against but for the fact that other painters copy the originator if he is successful. I am not in favour of following any particular school, because it only results in being copied by supporters . . .

The young Picasso's wish was granted when, four years later, he was given an exhibition of his works in Paris.

After years of Spanish-found inspiration, there is little doubt about the role played by the French in fertilizing the seedbed of Spanish self-fulfillment. Through France, Spanish composers came to develop and enhance the long-cherished traditional music that surrounded them and one of the world's greatest artists found recognition and support. And, in the long history of French fascination for Spain, no feedback could have been more felicitous.

Contemporary composers

Emmanuel Chabrier (1841-1894)

Chabrier studied the piano before moving to Paris where he became a civil servant. In 1879, he heard a performance of Wagner's *Tristan* which moved him to give up his job in order to compose music. He wrote mostly operas and piano works.

Luigi Cherubini (1760-1842)

Born in Florence, Italy, Cherubini had composed an oratorio, several Masses and choral works by the age of 16. He settled in Paris, but his fortunes fluctuated with the French Revolution and Napoleonic era. He became a superintendent for Louis XVIII's chapel and Director of the Paris Conservatoire in 1822. From 1837, he stopped composing in order to teach. One of his pupils was Halévy.

Paul Dukas (1865-1935)

Dukas entered the Paris Conservatoire when he was 16. His last major work, a ballet, was completed in 1912. He taught at the Conservatoire and was a noted critic and editor.

Gabriel Fauré (1845-1924)

Fauré was trained as a church musician and from 1861 was taught by Saint Saëns. Most of Fauré's music was religious. He was appointed Director of the Paris Conservatoire in 1905, but he was forced to resign in 1920 because of deafness.

César Franck (1822-1890)

Franck, with the enthusiastic backing of his father, completed a concert tour at the age of 11. In 1837, Franck entered the Paris Conservatoire, where he became a professor in 1872. D'Indy, Debussy and Bizet were among his pupils.

Jacques Halévy (1799-1862)

Halévy entered the Paris Conservatoire in 1809 and became a professor there in 1840. His pupils included Gounod and Bizet. He completed 24 operas before dying of consumption in 1862.

Arthur Honegger (1892-1955)

Honegger studied at the Zurich and Paris Conservatoires and in 1920 was included in *Les Six* (a group of six 'anti-Romantic' composers who revered Satie). Honegger's works consisted of operas, oratorios, ballets and film scores.

Alexandre Charles Lecocq (1832-1918)

Lecocq was physically handicapped from birth, but studied the organ at the Paris Conservatoire, where one of his teachers was Halévy. In 1856, he won a competition sponsored by Offenbach.

Jules Massenet (1842-1912)

In 1851, Massenet entered the Paris Conservatoire, to study piano. He later became the youngest member of the Académie Française and was eventually made its President.

Darius Milhaud (1892-1974)

Milhaud entered the Paris Conservatoire in 1909. He was named as one of *Les Six* in 1920. His work was prolific and varied, including symphonies, choral works and film scores. He also taught in California.

Francis Poulenc (1899-1963)

Although Poulenc had had piano lessons, he was mostly self-taught when he was included in *Les Six*. His output was large and, after 1936, much of it was religious.

Camille Saint-Saëns (1835-1921)

Saint-Saëns gave public piano recitals from an early age and entered the Paris Conservatoire at 13 where he studied with Halévy. Although elected a member of the Académic Française, his work was more popular in England.

The Strauss Brothers

Josef (1827-1870) was younger than Johann II and, although as talented, he wanted to be an engineer. He did take over the family orchestra whenever it was necessary, however.

Eduard (1835-1916), though competent as a composer, was less inspired than Josef. He became a popular conductor with the family orchestra.

Bibliography

Bernac, P. *Francis Poulenc: The Man and His Songs.* Norton (New York, 1978).

Davies, L. *Franck: The Man and His Circle.* Da Capo (New York, 1977).

Harding J. *Jacques Offenbach: a Biography.* Riverrun (New York, 1981).

Noske, F. *French Song from Berlioz to Duparc.* Trans. Rita Benton. Dover (New York, 1987).

Orenstein, A. *Ravel.* Columbia University Press (New York, 1975).

Rich, A. *The Simon & Schuster's Listener's Guide to Opera.* Simon & Schuster (New York, 1980).

Vallas, L. *Claude Debussy: His Life and Works.* Trans. Marie and Grace O'Brien. Dover (New York, 1973).

Walsh, T. *Second Empire Opera.* Riverrun (New York, 1980).

Wechsberg, J. *The Waltz Emperors: The Life and Times and Music of the Strauss Family.* Putnam (New York, 1973).

Wenk, A. *Claude Debussy and the Poets.* University of California Press (Berkeley, 1976).

Index